Living Free

Living Free

A Christ-Centered Twelve Step Program

Jimmy R. Lee

BAKER BOOK HOUSE
Grand Rapids, Michigan 49516

© 1993 by Jimmy Ray Lee

Published by Baker Books,
a division of Baker Book House Company
P.O. Box 6287, Grand Rapids, Michigan 49516-6287

ISBN: 0-8010-5680-2

Printed in the United States of America

Twelve Steps of Alcoholics Anonymous

1. We admitted we were powerless over alcohol—that our lives had become unmanageable.
2. Came to believe that a Power greater than ourselves could restore us to sanity.
3. Made a decision to turn our will and our lives over to the care of God *as we understood Him.*
4. Made a searching and fearless moral inventory of ourselves.
5. Admitted to God, to ourselves and to another human being the exact nature of our wrongs.
6. Were entirely ready to have God remove all these defects of character.
7. Humbly asked Him to remove our shortcomings.
8. Made a list of all persons we had harmed, and became willing to make amends to them all.
9. Made direct amends to such people wherever possible, except when to do so would injure them or others.
10. Continued to take personal inventory and when we were wrong, promptly admitted it.
11. Sought through prayer and meditation to improve our conscious contact with God *as we understood Him,* praying only for knowledge of His will for us and the power to carry that out.
12. Having had a spiritual awakening as the result of these steps, we tried to carry this message to alcoholics, and to practice these principles in all our affairs.

Acknowledgments

The author is thankful to Dr. Gary R. Sweeten and Hal B. Schell for the use of "The Twelve Steps of Wholeness." The material is published by permission of:

Equipping Ministries International
4015 Executive Park Drive, Suite 309
Cincinnati, OH 45241
(513) 769-5353

Contents

Part One
A Personal Guide

Introduction

Welcome to *Living Free*. This is a twelve-step approach to becoming free in Christ. The twelve steps used in *Living Free* are taken from "The Twelve Steps of Wholeness" by Gary R. Sweeten and Hal B. Schell.

They explain: "Following a tradition of the early church and the Wesley revival, the Oxford Group systematized a series of 'steps' as a process of cleansing one's inner life. These 'steps' were later adapted by Alcoholics Anonymous with much of the Christian basis ignored. They are here re-adapted emphasizing this great Christian base so integral to the wholeness sought. Here the center of wholeness is recognized as the Lord Jesus Christ. The 'steps' have also been changed to conform to other principles of discipleship and Christian growth."

The purpose of *Living Free* is to help you develop roots and steadfastness in Christ so that you can confidently master the problems you encounter. If you have not received Christ as your Savior, we invite you to make this important decision. Please see page 167.

Living Free is not a substitute for medical or psychological care. We never advise anyone to stop taking medication or cancel a physician's care.

Please be faithful in your attendance at each group meeting and do the Learning Assignment before each group session. There is a Step-by-Step Diary page for you to record your thoughts after each session.

May the Lord bless you and keep his hand on you.

Jimmy R. Lee

Step 12: Advancing My Faith in Christ

Step 11: Anchoring My Walk with Christ

Step 10: Analyzing My Walk with Christ

Step 9: Acting on My Amends

Step 8: Amending My Ways

Step 7: Abandoning My Sins

Step 6: Agreeing with God

Step 5: Accounting for My Actions

Step 4: Auditing My Life

Step 3: Affirming My Need for the Care of God

Step 2: Acknowledging My Belief in Jesus Christ

Step 1: Admitting My Powerlessness

The Twelve Steps of Wholeness

If a Christian will vigorously apply these principles, and make these decisions, that person will move toward "Teleios"— Wholeness in Christ.

1. I now see that I, of myself, am powerless, unable to control (manage) my life by myself.

   Romans 7 and 8   Romans 7:18–19   Psalm 32:3–7
                            Romans 3:9–10, 23

2. I now realize that my Creator, God the Father, Son, and Holy Spirit, can restore me to wholeness in Christ.

   Psalm 27:4–5   Mark 10:26–27   Philippians 2:13
   Romans 8:9   Ezekiel 36:27

3. I now make a conscious decision to turn my entire will and life over to the care and direction of Jesus Christ as Teacher, Healer, Savior, and Lord.

   Joshua 1:8–9   Jeremiah 29:11–14   Jeremiah 32:27
   John 14:6   John 10:30   Mark 10:27
   Matthew 28:18, 20b

4. Having made this decision, I now obey God's call in Scripture to make a fearless, ethical, moral, and scriptural inventory of my entire life in order to uncover all sins, mistakes, and character defects, and to make a written list of every item uncovered.

   Psalm 139:23–24   Lamentations 3:40   Jeremiah 23:24
   Romans 8:26–27

5. After completing this inventory I now will to "walk in the light, as he is in the light" by admitting to myself, to God, and to at least one other person in Christ the exact nature of these wrongs.

Psalm 119:9–11   Acts 13:38–39   1 Timothy 1:15
James 5:13–16   Ephesians 5:13–14   Hebrews 9:14
1 John 1:7   Acts 2:37–38

6. Having agreed with God about my sinful behavior, I now ask his forgiveness through Christ and openly acknowledge that I am forgiven according to Scripture.

James 4:10   1 John 1:8–9   1 John 2:1–2
Psalm 27:13–14   Psalm 118:18, then 17

7. I now repent (turn away) from all these behaviors in thought, word, and deed, and ask God to remove each besetting sin, through Jesus Christ.

John 5:14   John 8:10–11   Job 11:13–19
Ezekiel 18:30–32   Romans 5 and 6   Romans 12:1–2
1 John 2:3–6   2 Corinthians 10:5   Colossians 3:17

8. I now make a list of all persons I have harmed in thought, word, and deed, and a list of all persons I believe have harmed me, and will to make amends to all of them.

Ephesians 4:29–32   Hosea 11:1–4   Ephesians 5:1–2
Luke 6:31   Matthew 5:43–44   Matthew 18:15
Leviticus 19:17–18   Mark 12:31   Matthew 5:9

9. I now go directly to these persons to forgive and to seek forgiveness, reconciliation, restitution, or release whenever and with whomever possible, unless to do so would cause further harm.

Matthew 5:23–24   Isaiah 1:18–20

10. I now consciously and prayerfully continue to "walk in the light" by unceasingly taking personal inventory of all my temptations and sins, and by keeping a constantly open relationship with God, myself, and other persons.

Matthew 26:41	James 1:13–15	Matthew 6:11–13
Proverbs 30:8–9	Ephesians 5:15–18	Ephesians 4:22–28
Psalm 4:3–5	Psalm 55:22	1 Peter 5:6–7
Colossians 3:13		

11. I now continue in regular Scripture study, prayer, worship, and fellowship to increase God's will in my life.

Acts 2:42	Mark 12:28–33	Matthew 6:33
Psalm 89:15	Joshua 1:8	1 Kings 8:56–61
	Colossians 3:12–17	

12. Recognizing the impact of God in my life, I now intentionally share these principles and their effect with others as God's Spirit leads, and will to practice these principles in all areas of my life.

Micah 6:8	Ephesians 5:8	Psalm 40:8–10
Galatians 5:1	Revelation 12:11	2 Corinthians 3:17
	Ephesians 6:10–18	

Prepared by Dr. Gary R. Sweeten and Hal B. Schell, © 1989 Equipping Ministries International, Inc., 4015 Executive Park Drive, Suite 309, Cincinnati, Ohio 45241. Used by permission.

Session 1

Admitting My Powerlessness

Step 1   I now see [admit] that I, of myself, am powerless, unable to control [manage] my life by myself.

Pre-session Learning Assignment

1. Introduction

Take 30 minutes each day to be alone with God in meditation and prayer. Read Romans 7 and 8. What do these Scripture passages mean to you, and how do they apply to your life?

2. Self-awareness

The first step of recovery for a person suffering with a life-controlling problem(s) is to admit he/she is powerless over the problem. A life-controlling problem is anything that masters a person's life (see 1 Cor. 6:12).

Everybody has the potential of being mastered by a life-controlling substance, behavior, or another person. Admitting our powerlessness is not a weakness, it is a strength. List by name(s) the life-controlling problem(s) or the developing of a life-controlling problem that is causing you concern. This is for your own personal reflection.

3. Spiritual Awareness

Read Romans 7:18–8:2. The apostle Paul recognized his powerlessness to carry out good desires without the help of Jesus Christ. It is important to recognize our powerlessness, because only then are we free to turn our life-controlling problems over to God.

Check Box When Read	
☐ Romans 7:18–20	Paul recognized his own powerlessness.
☐ Romans 7:21–24	Paul recognized a war in his inner being.
☐ Romans 7:25–8:2	Paul recognized that the only way to deal with his powerlessness was through Jesus Christ.
☐ Romans 3:23	All are guilty of sin.
☐ Psalm 6:6–7 ☐ Psalm 31 ☐ Proverbs 28:26 ☐ Romans 3:9–10	

4. Application

The apostle Paul writes (2 Cor. 12:9–10), "But he [Jesus] said to me, 'My grace is sufficient for you, for my power is made perfect in weakness.' Therefore I will boast all the more gladly about my weaknesses, so that Christ's power may rest on me. . . . For when I am weak, then I am strong."

Describe an event or situation in your life that helped you recognize your need for God. How can you apply these Scriptures to your personal weakness?

Notes

Step-by-Step Diary
Step 1

Session 2

Acknowledging My Belief in Jesus Christ

Step 2 *I now realize that my Creator, God the
Father, Son, and Holy Spirit, can restore me to wholeness in Christ.*

Pre-session Learning Assignment

1. Introduction

Take 30 minutes each day to be alone with God in meditation
and prayer. Read Philippians 1–4. What do these Scripture passages mean to you, and how do they apply to your life?

2. Self-awareness

To effectively deal with a life-controlling problem(s) a person
needs help from a greater power. We have access to God only
through Jesus Christ his Son (see John 14:6).

It is possible for a person to trust in his/her own self-will or develop a false belief system based on his/her own ability or an incorrect concept of God. In what ways have you tried to manage your own life?

What kind of feelings do you experience from trying to deal with a life-controlling problem within the sphere of your own strength?

3. Spiritual Awareness

Read Philippians 2:12–13. God works in us to fulfill his purpose for our life. As God works in us, we are responsible to work out our own salvation with reverence and respect for him, refraining from those things that might discredit the name of Christ.

Check Box When Read		
☐ Philippians 2:12	We are to work out our salvation with fear and trembling (as God works in us).	
☐ Philippians 2:13	God works in us to fulfill his purpose.	
☐ Romans 10:9–10	Exercising faith in Jesus Christ is vital.	
☐ Psalm 46:1	God is always available to help.	
☐ Psalm 27:4–5	☐ Psalm 34:18–22	☐ Isaiah 12:2
☐ Ezekiel 36:27	☐ Mark 9:23–24	☐ Mark 10:26–27
☐ John 8:32	☐ John 15:5	☐ Romans 8:9
☐ 2 Corinthians 1:9	☐ Ephesians 3:20	☐ Hebrews 11:6

4. Application

How would you describe your relationship with Jesus Christ?

At what times is it most difficult for you to place your trust in Jesus Christ?

Fill in **Identifying Goals** list on page 24.

IDENTIFYING GOALS		
Goals for My:	My Part	God's Part
Church		
Family		
Career		
Personal Needs		
Education		
Physical Needs		
	My Responsibility Continue to work out your salvation with fear and trembling (Phil. 2:12).	**God's Responsibility** For it is God who works in you to will and to act according to his good purpose (Phil. 2:13).

Notes

Step-by-Step Diary

Step 2

Session 3

Affirming My Need for the Care of God

Step 3 I now make a conscious decision to turn my entire will and life over to the care and direction of Jesus Christ as Teacher, Healer, Savior, and Lord.

Pre-session Learning Assignment

1. Introduction

Take 30 minutes each day to be alone with God in meditation and prayer. Read Romans 12–14. What do these Scripture passages mean to you, and how do they apply to your life?

2. Self-awareness

Making a decision to turn his/her life over to God through Jesus Christ is extremely important for the person dealing with a life-controlling problem(s). The commitment is twofold: (1) a commitment to turn his/her will and life over to God; (2) a commitment to not be mastered by any substance, behavior or personal relationship. The control is turned over to the *care of God.* Can you think of ways you have resisted God's will for your life? Explain.

How do you feel about your decision to give up control of your life to the care of God?

3. Spiritual Awareness

Read Romans 12:1–2. It is God's will that a person surrender his/her life over to God's direction. God is pleased when a person resists the pressure to be squeezed into the world's pattern.

Check Box When Read		
☐ Romans 12:1	We are encouraged to present ourselves to God.	
☐ Romans 12:2	We are to guard against the pressures of this world.	
☐ Romans 12:2	God has a perfect will for everyone.	
☐ Proverbs 3:5–6	We are encouraged to trust in the Lord.	
☐ Joshua 1:8–9	☐ Psalm 118: 8–9	☐ Proverbs 16:3
☐ Isaiah 30:15	☐ Isaiah 55:6–7	☐ Jeremiah 29:11–14
☐ Jeremiah 32:27	☐ Mark 10:27	☐ John 1:12–13
☐ John 10:29–30	☐ John 14:6	☐ Galatians 2:20
☐ Revelation 3:20		

4. Application

A meaningful decision requires action on our part. What actions will accompany your decision to turn your life over to the care of God?

How will you deal with the tendency to regain control of your life?

Notes

Step-by-Step Diary
Step 3

Session 4

Auditing My Life

Step 4   *Having made this decision, I now obey God's call in Scripture to make a fearless, ethical, moral, and scriptural inventory of my entire life in order to uncover all sins, mistakes, and character defects, and to make a written list of every item uncovered.*

Pre-session Learning Assignment

1. Introduction

Take 30 minutes each day to be alone with God in meditation and prayer. Read Psalm 139–150. What do these Scripture passages mean to you, and how do they apply to your life?

2. Self-awareness

As a person continues to build a foundation for his/her recovery it is important for him/her to search with honesty all aspects of his/her life. Excuses for inappropriate behavior should be dismissed.

As you search yourself please remember that God will direct your life. As you conduct your personal audit prepare a written list of items that are uncovered. This will help you focus on the need and surface those items that need to be placed in God's care. This written list is for your personal reflection. See **Personal Audit** on page 35.

In what ways can a personal examination help you look to God for help?

3. Spiritual Awareness

Read Psalm 139:1–4, 23–24. David recognized the need for God to search his heart.

Check Box When Read	
☐ Psalm 139:1–2	The Lord knows us personally.
☐ Psalm 139:3–4	The Lord knows our actions.
☐ Psalm 139:23–24	David was open to personal examination.
☐ Lamentations 3:40	Restoration includes personal examination and testing.
☐ Jeremiah 17:9–10	Jeremiah describes the heart as deceitful.
☐ Jeremiah 23:24	☐ Lamentations 3:19–23 ☐ John 6:68–69
☐ John 14:26	☐ John 16:13 ☐ Romans 8:26–27
☐ 2 Corinthians 13:5–6	☐ James 1:12

4. Application

David is described as a man after God's own heart (Acts 13:22). He was open to personal examination before the Lord. What lessons can you learn from David in conducting your own inventory?

How do you feel about God knowing you on a personal basis?

Personal Audit

My relationship with God:

My relationship with my family:

My relationship with my church:

My relationship with my friends:

Memory Verse

Search me, O God, and know my heart; test me and know my anxious thoughts (Ps. 139:23).

Notes

Step-by-Step Diary
Step 4

Session 5

Accounting for My Actions

Step 5   *After completing this inventory I now will to "walk in the light, as he is in the light" by admitting to myself, to God, and to at least one other person in Christ the exact nature of these wrongs.*

Pre-session Learning Assignment

1. Introduction

Take 30 minutes each day to be alone with God in meditation and prayer. Read 1 John 1–5. What do these Scripture passages mean to you, and how do they apply to your life?

2. Self-awareness

It can be helpful for a person to admit to himself/herself, God, and others his/her written list of items that need to be placed in God's care. Sharing with others helps remove the person from isolation caused by the wall of defenses used to protect the stronghold. Although it may be helpful for you to share your concerns with another person who is *mature in Christ*, remember—only Christ can forgive sins. There may be some personal items that need to be discussed *only with the Lord.*

In what ways have you felt isolation because of a life-controlling problem(s)?

With whom do you feel comfortable in sharing your concerns? Why did you select this person?

3. Spiritual Awareness

Read 1 John 1:5–10 and 1 John 2:1–2. Walking in the light results in true fellowship with God and each other. As we admit our sins and confess them to Jesus, we are forgiven through his blood.

Accounting for My Actions

Check Box When Read	
☐ 1 John 1:5–6	God is light and truth.
☐ 1 John 1:7	Walking in the light results in fellowship with God and one another.
☐ 1 John 1:8–10	There is a cause and remedy for deceit.
☐ 1 John 2:1–2	Jesus is the mediator between God and man.
☐ James 5:16	Confession and prayer are vital to the healing process.

☐ Psalm 119:9–11	☐ Proverbs 28:13	☐ Jeremiah 14:20
☐ Acts 2:37–38	☐ Acts 3:19	☐ Acts 13:38–39
☐ Romans 3:23	☐ Romans 14:12	☐ Ephesians 5:13–14
☐ 1 Timothy 1:15	☐ Hebrews 9:14	

4. Application

When we receive Christ as Savior our sins are forgiven and nailed to the cross through Christ (see Col. 2:13–15). After you have shared your personal items (within your own comfort level) with a mature Christian, destroy your written list (**Personal Audit**) as an act of praise to the Lord. Write a prayer of thanksgiving.

There are things on the written list that only God can deal with. However, there may be items on the list that need continued prayer and corrective action on your part. Describe this for your own personal reflection.

Prayer List

Person and/or Situation   Request

Notes

Step-by-Step Diary

Step 5

Session 6

Agreeing with God

Step 6 *Having agreed with God about my sinful behavior, I now ask his forgiveness through Christ and openly acknowledge that I am forgiven according to Scripture.*

Pre-session Learning Assignment

1. Introduction

Take 30 minutes each day to be alone with God in meditation and prayer. Read James 1–5. What do these Scripture passages mean to you, and how do they apply to your life?

2. Self-awareness

It is important for a person to continue his/her denouncement of sin and focus on *walking out* the changes in his/her life. He/She should continue to be on the alert for denial and delusion, asking the Lord to give him/her clear thinking so he/she can follow him.

What actions are you taking to confront negative trends of behavior? This is for your own personal reflection.

How have negative trends of behavior affected your self-esteem?

3. Spiritual Awareness

Read Amos 3:3 and James 4:7–10. Agreeing with God and walking with God go hand in hand. It is impossible to walk with God without being in agreement with him.

Check Box When Read		
☐ Amos 3:3	Walking with God means harmony.	
☐ James 4:7–8	Walking with God means submission.	
☐ James 4:9–10	Walking with God means humility.	
☐ Ephesians 1:7	Walking with God means that I agree with God that I am forgiven of my sins.	
☐ Jude 21 (TLB)	Walking with God means that I am walking within his boundaries.	
☐ Psalm 27:13–14	☐ Psalm 37:4–5	☐ Psalm 118:17–18
☐ Psalm 119:11	☐ Proverbs 19:21	☐ Proverbs 21:30–31
☐ Isaiah 1:18–19	☐ Romans 6:11–14	☐ 2 Thessalonians 3:3
☐ Hebrews 4:16		

45

4. Application

What outward changes are occurring in your life as a result of your commitment to agree with God and to allow him to manage your life?

What areas of self-management have been the most difficult for you to turn over to God? This is for your own personal reflection.

Notes

Step-by-Step Diary
Step 6

Session 7

Abandoning My Sins

Step 7 *I now repent (turn away) from all these behaviors in thought, word, and deed, and ask God to remove each besetting sin, through Jesus Christ.*

Pre-session Learning Assignment

1. Introduction

Take 30 minutes each day to be alone with God in meditation and prayer. Read Hebrews 11–13. What do these Scripture passages mean to you, and how do they apply to your life?

2. Self-awareness

As a person continues to *walk out* changes in his/her life there should always be a focus on *turning from* his/her sin. Secret sins need to be admitted and confessed to Christ.

These shortcomings should be approached with an attitude of surrender. Having confessed them to Christ, now is the time to submit to his purifying process through obedience.

What character defects do you continue to struggle with? This is for your own personal reflection.

What is your definition of repentance?

3. Spiritual Awareness

Read Hebrews 12:1–3. Repentance (turning away from our sins) and faith in Jesus Christ are vital to our recovery. Repentance and faith in Jesus Christ go hand in hand in the recovery process.

Check Box When Read	
☐ Hebrews 12:1	We are encouraged to deal with "everything that hinders" us.
☐ Hebrews 12:2	We are encouraged to focus our attention on Jesus.
☐ Hebrews 12:3	We are encouraged to consider the endurance of Jesus.
☐ Acts 26:20	Repentance is proved by our deeds.
☐ Acts 3:19	Repentance brings a refreshing from the Lord.
☐ Job 11:13–19	☐ Psalm 51:10	☐ Psalm 90:8
☐ Psalm 103:2–3	☐ Ezekiel 18:30–32	☐ Daniel 4:27
☐ John 5:14	☐ John 8:10–11	☐ Acts 20:21
☐ Romans 5 and 6	☐ Romans 12:1–2	☐ 2 Corinthians 2:10
☐ 2 Corinthians 10:5	☐ Philippians 4:6	☐ Colossians 3:17
☐ 1 Peter 5:6–7	☐ 1 John 2:3–6	

4. Application

Solomon writes (Prov. 3:5–6), "Trust in the LORD with all your heart and lean not on your own understanding; in all your ways acknowledge him, and he will make your paths straight." How do you plan to apply these verses to your life to deal with hindrances to your walk in Christ?

In what ways have you *leaned on your own understanding?*

Notes

Step-by-Step Diary
Step 7

Session 8

Amending My Ways

Step 8 I now make a list of all persons I have harmed in thought, word, and deed, and a list of all persons I believe have harmed me, and will to make amends to all of them.

Pre-session Learning Assignment

1. Introduction

Take 30 minutes each day to be alone with God in meditation and prayer. Read 2 Corinthians 5–9. What do these Scripture passages mean to you, and how do they apply to your life?

2. Self-awareness

As a person breaks out of delusion and becomes aware of the reality of his/her situation, he/she may now be sensitive of others who may have been harmed by his/her behaviors. Continuing to cover up or blame others for his/her problems can result in further delusion and bitterness. Forgiving ourselves and others through Christ helps us overcome the past.

Make a list of persons you have harmed. This is for your own personal reflection. See **Amends** on page 57.

Make a list of persons you believe have harmed you. This is for your own personal reflection.

Can you think of past misdeeds that you cannot correct and have turned over to God? This is for your own personal reflection.

3. Spiritual Awareness

Read 2 Corinthians 5:17–21. Through Christ we have the ministry of reconciliation. This is possible because we have been reconciled to God through Christ.

Check Box When Read		
☐ 2 Corinthians 5:17	Being in Christ helps us deal with the past.	
☐ 2 Corinthians 5:18	Reconciliation comes through Christ.	
☐ 2 Corinthians 5:19	Our sins are not held against us.	
☐ 2 Corinthians 5:20	We are ambassadors for Christ.	
☐ 2 Corinthians 5:21	Our identity is in Christ.	
☐ Matthew 6:14–15	Forgiving ourselves and others is vital to our recovery.	
☐ Leviticus 19:17–18	☐ Psalm 19:13–14	☐ Psalm 32:1–2
☐ Hosea 11:1–4	☐ Matthew 5:9	☐ Matthew 5:43–45
☐ Matthew 18:21–35	☐ Mark 12:31	☐ Luke 6:31
☐ Ephesians 4:29–32	☐ Colossians 3:13	☐ 1 John 4:7–12

4. Application

In view of Jesus' statement, "Do to others as you would have them do to you" (Luke 6:31), how do you plan your approach in amending broken or strained relationships?

How are you dealing with forgiving yourself?

How are you dealing with forgiving others?

Amends

Person　　　Relationship　　　Actions to Correct

Notes

Step-by-Step Diary
Step 8

Session 9

Acting on My Amends

Step 9   *I now go directly to those persons to forgive and to seek forgiveness, reconciliation, restitution, or release whenever and with whomever possible, unless to do so would cause further harm.*

Pre-session Learning Assignment

1. Introduction

Take 30 minutes each day to be alone with God in meditation and prayer. Read Matthew 5–7 and Luke 15. What do these Scripture passages mean to you, and how do they apply to your life?

2. Self-awareness

It can be helpful for a person to go directly to those who may have been harmed by strained or broken relationships. It is important to seek God's wisdom and timing in seeking forgiveness and reconciliation. A person should approach only those with whom he/she has access and would not cause further harm. (Further harm includes areas that may cause damage which would be beyond repair.) Describe strained or broken relationships with people in which you have accessibility. This is for your own personal reflection.

Can these people be approached without causing further harm? If so, how?

3. Spiritual Awareness

Read Matthew 5:23–24 and Luke 15:18–24. Jesus encourages us to amend strained or broken relationships with others. Those relationships that cannot be restored because of inaccessibility or likely further harm should be released to the Lord's care.

Check Box When Read	
☐ Matthew 5:23–24	We are encouraged to make peace with our brother.
☐ Luke 15:18–21	The prodigal son made peace with his father and heaven.
☐ 1 Peter 5:7	God helps us with those relationships that are beyond our control.

☐ Numbers 5:5–7	☐ Isaiah 1:18–20	☐ Ezekiel 33:15–16
☐ Luke 6:35	☐ Romans 12:17–18	☐ Ephesians 5:21
☐ Philippians 2:3–4	☐ 1 Thessalonians 5:11	

4. Application

Describe a difficult situation(s) that you might face in your effort to make amends in strained or broken relationships.

In what ways can your support group help you?

In what ways can you help support others in this group?

Notes

Step-by-Step Diary
Step 9

Session 10

Analyzing My Walk with Christ

*Step 10 I now consciously and prayerfully
continue to "walk in the light" by
unceasingly taking personal inventory
of all my temptations and sins, and by
keeping a constantly open relationship
with God, myself, and other persons.*

Pre-session Learning Assignment

1. Introduction

Take 30 minutes each day to be alone with God in meditation
and prayer. Read 1 Corinthians 10 and 2 Corinthians 1–3.
What do these Scripture passages mean to you, and how do they
apply to your life?

2. Self-awareness

It is helpful for a person to discuss victories and gains made. However, he/she should also be aware of his/her weakness to relapse into the former life-style. There are various triggering devices that can lead to relapse. These triggering devices include:

Socializing with former friends who have a negative influence.
Withdrawing from church services and support group.
"Talking the talk" but not "walking the walk."
Going to places that have a negative influence.
Avoiding those who are concerned friends.

How are you dealing with the above triggering devices?

Can you think of other triggering devices that are not listed? Describe.

3. Spiritual Awareness

Read 1 Corinthians 10:12–13 and 2 Corinthians 3:4–6. It is important to place our confidence in Christ (not our own accomplishments). It is helpful to be open with the Lord about the temptations which can hinder our walk with him.

Check Box When Read	
☐ 1 Corinthians 10:12	Paul warns against being overconfident.
☐ 1 Corinthians 10:13	Paul shows how to deal with temptation.
☐ 2 Corinthians 3:4–6	Our confidence should be in Christ, not in our own resources.
☐ James 1:13–15	God does not tempt us.

☐ Psalm 4:3–5	☐ Psalm 34:12–14	☐ Psalm 55:22
☐ Psalm 139:1–4	☐ Proverbs 30:8–9	☐ Galatians 6:4–5
☐ Ephesians 4:25–26	☐ James 1:23–25	

4. Application

Describe your progress at this point.

What does an open relationship with God mean to you?

What areas in your life do you still struggle with?

Notes

Step-by-Step Diary
Step 10

Session 11

Anchoring My Walk with Christ

***Step 11** I now continue in regular Scripture study, prayer, worship, and fellowship to increase God's will in my life.*

Pre-session Learning Assignment

1. Introduction

Take 30 minutes each day to be alone with God in meditation and prayer. Read Colossians 1–4. What do these Scripture passages mean to you, and how do they apply to your life?

2. Self-awareness

Turning one's life over to God is a vital decision. Next, a person should focus on the continuity of his/her walk with the Lord. It is important to practice regular times of prayer and meditation. This will help a person direct his/her thoughts to God and his will for his/her life.

How are you dealing with negative thoughts?

What do you think will happen if you permit negative thoughts to linger in your mind?

How do you feel about your personal need to meditate on God and his Word?

3. Spiritual Awareness

Read Colossians 3:12–17. God wants to direct our lives on a daily basis through prayer, study, and meditation of his Word. Paul shows us how God can influence our daily inventory of thoughts and actions.

Check Box When Read	
☐ Colossians 3:12	As God's chosen people we are to clothe ourselves with his garments.
☐ Colossians 3:13	We are to forgive each other.
☐ Colossians 3:14	Love and perfect unity go hand in hand.
☐ Colossians 3:15	The "peace of Christ" plays an important role in directing our lives.
☐ Colossians 3:16	We are encouraged to let the "word of Christ dwell in us."
☐ Colossians 3:17	We are encouraged to do all "in the name of the Lord Jesus."

☐ Joshua 1:8	☐ 1 Kings 8:56–61	☐ Psalm 1:1–3
☐ Psalm 19:14	☐ Psalm 25:1–5	☐ Psalm 63:1–7
☐ Psalm 89:15	☐ Isaiah 30:21	☐ Matthew 6:33–34
☐ Matthew 7:7	☐ Mark 11:24	☐ Mark 12:28–33
☐ Acts 2:42	☐ Philippians 4:6–9	

4. Application

Describe your present schedule for your personal devotions.

How do you feel about your persistence?

How do you deal with interruptions?

Notes

Step-by-Step Diary
Step 11

Session 12

Advancing My Faith in Christ

Step 12 Recognizing the impact of God in my life, I now intentionally share these principles and their effect with others as God's Spirit leads, and will to practice these principles in all areas of my life.

Pre-session Learning Assignment

1. Introduction

Take 30 minutes each day to be alone with God in meditation and prayer. Read 1 Peter 1–5. What do these Scripture passages mean to you, and how do they apply to your life?

2. Self-awareness

Although this course brings a person to a point of completion, his/her walk with Christ is not complete. It is important for a person to continue to practice the principles presented in this study. As a person continues to focus on *walking out* the truth learned and applied in this course, he/she should focus on reaching out to others who are hurting. As he/she shares with others what the Lord is doing in his/her life the Lord will bless him/her.

In what ways do you feel responsible to share with others?

Describe any anxiety you might have about sharing Christ with others.

Describe a significant person(s) God used in helping you. In what ways did this person(s) help you?

3. Spiritual Awareness

Read 1 Peter 3:15–18. Peter encourages us to share the hope that we have in Christ. We should always be prepared to share our faith with others.

Check Box When Read	
☐ 1 Peter 3:15	Christ should always have a special place in our hearts; we should be prepared "to give the reason for the hope" we have.
☐ 1 Peter 3:16	We are to maintain "a clear conscience."
☐ 1 Peter 3:17	God's will for our lives may include suffering.
☐ 1 Peter 3:18	Christ died for our sins.
☐ Proverbs 24:11; ☐ Jude 22–23	We are to help those being led to the way of death.

☐ Psalm 40:8–10	☐ Isaiah 61:1–3	☐ Jeremiah 20:9
☐ Micah 6:8	☐ Matthew 28:19–20	☐ Mark 5:19
☐ Luke 4:18–19	☐ 2 Corinthians 3:17–18	☐ Galatians 5:1
☐ Galatians 6:1–5	☐ Ephesians 5:8–10	☐ Ephesians 6:10–18
☐ Colossians 4:5–6	☐ Revelation 12:11	

4. Application

Paul writes (2 Cor. 1:3–4), "Praise be to the God and Father of our Lord Jesus Christ, the Father of compassion and the God of all comfort, who comforts us in all our troubles, so that we can comfort those in any trouble with the comfort we ourselves have received from God."

Why do you think it is important to share the comfort we have received from the Lord with others?

How will you depend on the Holy Spirit to guide you?

Notes

Step-by-Step Diary
Step 12

Follow-up

Where Do I Go from Here?

Goal Setting

1. *Three Goals for My Life*

A.

B.

C.

2. *Submitting My Goals to God's Care and Direction*

Trust in the LORD with all your heart and lean not on your own understanding; in all your ways acknowledge him, and he will make your paths straight (Prov. 3:5–6).

Ways I will trust the Lord and lean on him for understanding to achieve my goals:

Goal A:

Goal B:

Goal C:

Ways I will acknowledge him to direct my life to achieve my goals:

Goal A:

Goal B:

Goal C:

3. Areas I Need to Work on to Achieve My Goals

Goal A:

Goal B:

Goal C:

4. I Recognize That God's Purpose for My Life May Change My Goals

Many are the plans in a man's heart, but it is the LORD's purpose that prevails (Prov. 19:21).

My Prayer of Submission:

Memory Verse

For I know the plans I have for you, declares the LORD, plans to prosper you and not to harm you, plans to give you hope and a future (Jer. 29:11).

Part Two
A Facilitator's Group Guide

Suggested Group Format

Getting Started

We suggest that the group have two group leaders (facilitators) and a maximum of twelve group participants. Having more than twelve may prevent some from being a part of the much needed discussion.

The facilitators should meet prior to each group session to pray and make final plans for the session. They should also meet after each session to discuss what happened during the meeting and discuss any follow-up that is needed.

In the orientation session, *Living Free,* containing "learning assignments" for Steps 1–12, should be distributed to each group member. Facilitators should have a thorough understanding of the workbook before distributing it to group participants. Encourage group members to complete the appropriate "learning assignment" prior to each group meeting; this prepares them for the upcoming session. Follow this format for each session.

The facilitators should be familiar with the suggested group format since this is the pattern in which the curriculum should be presented. Note that in the spiritual awareness part of each session there are statements and questions regarding certain biblical passages and sometimes general questions concerning the subject being presented. These same statements are listed in the *Facilitator's Group Guide* but without the questions. These questions are not asked in the *Facilitator's Group Guide* in order to enhance the spontaneity of the group process.

The small group format for each session consists of four phases: Introduction, Self-awareness, Spiritual Awareness, and Application. There is a reason for each phase. The facilitators should plan each session with this format in mind.

1. Introduction (10–15 minutes)

Begin with prayer. The facilitator may ask one of the group members to lead in prayer. After the prayer, use a go-around (sharing question) to help get the group at ease and relaxed for ministry. (Suggested sharing questions are listed in Part Three.) The lead facilitator should respond to the go-around first, followed by the co-facilitator. This causes the group members to feel safer in participating in the exercise. After the facilitators have shared, the group members will share one after another around the circle. Always remind group members that they are not expected to share if they do not wish to share. The rule is, everyone works within his/her comfort level.

The go-arounds are not for detailed conversation. Ask the group to keep comments brief. If a person is obviously in pain during the go-around, the facilitator should interrupt the go-around and have prayer for the person in pain. After prayer, the go-arounds may resume.

2. Self-awareness (20–25 minutes)

After the introduction phase (go-arounds) is completed, the facilitator will lead the group into the self-awareness phase. The facilitator may say, "Now it is time for our self-awareness. Tonight we are going to discuss . . ."

Self-awareness is a time to practice James 5:16: "Therefore confess your sins to each other and pray for each other so that you may be healed. The prayer of a righteous man is powerful and effective." It is important to stay on the subject matter. This is a time to focus on needs and healing, not to have a "martyr or pity party."

It is suggested in self-awareness that the facilitators ask the group members to share as they wish, unlike the go-around segment referred to in the introduction phase. This is because people are at various comfort levels, and they should not feel pressured to self-disclose if they are uncomfortable. As the group continues to meet, members will feel more and more comfortable in being a part of the discussion.

Remember, prayer is *always* in order. If, during this phase a group member is hurting, stop and pray. One of the facilitators may lead in prayer or ask another group member to lead the prayer. This says two things to the group member: (1) Each member is important, and (2) You care about each individual.

3. Spiritual Awareness (20–25 minutes)

After the self-awareness phase, the facilitator will lead the group in Bible study time. The facilitator may say, "Turn in your Bibles to. . . . Our discussion will be on . . ."

Having briefly explained the topic, the facilitator should assign Scriptures listed in the *Facilitator's Guide* to group members. When each Scripture is called by the facilitator, the group member should read the verse(s). After the verses are read, give time for discussion.

4. Application (25 minutes)

This phase is actually a continuation of Phase 3. Use the question for the appropriate session listed in the *Facilitator's Guide*. The facilitator may say, "For our application of the Scripture passage, I would like the group to discuss this question. . . ." Ask for volunteers to share reflections on the question. The facilitators should emphasize the importance of the group members applying biblical principles to their lives. Help for life-controlling problems begins with **right thinking,** "But be transformed by the renewing of your mind" (Rom. 12:2). Obedience to the Word should follow with **right behavior. Right feelings** will follow right thinking and right behavior.

Orientation

1. Introduction (10–15 minutes)

Opening prayer
Ask the group members to introduce themselves. This should be done as a go-around.

2. Self-awareness (20–25 minutes)

In this orientation session, review with the group members what will be expected of them regarding attendance, absences, confidentiality, etc. Encourage group members to call or notify one of the facilitators if they cannot attend a session. Also, discuss the format which will be used for each group session and elaborate on the goals of the *Living Free Group*. Explain that the goal is to help group members in their desire to maintain a life free from mastering problems by developing roots and steadfastness in Christ. Give each person an opportunity to share why they are in this group. This sharing helps develop trust—trust that you are there as a caring person—not to judge or condemn them.

Specific goals for this session are:

To emphasize that the *Living Free Group* is a non-threatening environment. Everyone works within their own comfort level.

To stress the importance of attending each group session.

To have group members report why they are in the group.

To stress the need for personal devotion time.

To stress the need for confidentiality.

To distribute the workbooks.

To instruct group members to complete the workbook prior to each group session. Advise group members of the "Step-by-Step Diary" provided in their workbook.

To explain the group format that will be used for each session (Introduction, Self-awareness, Spiritual Awareness, and Application).

Spiritual awareness lead-in question

In each session our spiritual awareness will be based on biblical principles which emphasize spiritual growth in Christ as the means to ongoing freedom from life-controlling problems. Colossians 2:6–8 serves as the launching pad for the 12 sessions that follow. Let's read the text together.

So then, just as you received Christ Jesus as Lord, continue to live in him, rooted and built up in him, strengthened in the faith as you were taught, and overflowing with thankfulness. See to it that no one takes you captive through hollow and deceptive philosophy, which depends on human tradition and the basic principles of this world rather than on Christ. (Col. 2:6–8)

What does this say to you about being spiritually aware?

3. Spiritual Awareness: Colossians 2:6–8 (20–25 minutes)

The main objective of this session is to use the aspects of the apostle Paul's instruction in Colossians 2:6–8 as the launching pad for the *Living Free Group*.

Aspects include

- Paul emphasizes the need for continuity in Christ (v. 6).
  How does a person receive Christ? (See Eph. 2:8–9 and p. 167.)

  Why is God's grace and faith in Christ important in your desire to be mature in Christ?

- Paul encourages us to be "rooted and built up in him, strengthened in the faith . . . and overflowing with thankfulness" (v. 7).
  Describe in your own words the four-phase process listed by Paul:
  1) Rooted

  2) Built up in him

  3) Strengthened in the faith

  4) Overflowing with thankfulness.

• Paul warns against deceptive philosophy (v. 8).
In view of this verse why is it important to guard against vain intellectualism and human philosophy as the means to your wholeness instead of Christ?

Help group members understand the significance of God's grace and faith in Christ as the foundation for the twelve sessions that will follow.

Assign Scripture references in Spiritual Awareness section to group members. The Scriptures should be read before the group and openly discussed as time permits. (Caution: Stay on the subject.)

4. Application (25 minutes)

Group discussion: In John 8:31–32 Jesus told the believing Jews, "If you hold to my teaching, you are really my disciples. Then you will know the truth, and the truth will set you free." In view of these verses how can you maintain a life of living free?

Session 1

Admitting My Powerlessness

Step 1   I now see [admit] that I, of myself, am powerless, unable to control [manage] my life by myself.

1. Introduction (10–15 minutes)

Opening prayer
Use a "present tense go-around" (see p. 157)
Read **Step 1** to the group

2. Self-awareness (20–25 minutes)

The general goal of this session is to help group members admit their powerlessness over a life-controlling problem. (A life-controlling problem is anything that masters a person's life—see 1 Cor. 6:12.) Admitting our powerlessness over a life-controlling problem(s) (or the developing of a life-controlling problem) is not a weakness, it is a strength. Emphasize that we all have the potential for a life-controlling problem(s). Facing the reality of a life-controlling problem may be difficult; however, it is the start on the road to recovery.

Specific goals for this session are:

To have group members specify (name) the life-controlling problem that they are struggling with: substance, behavior, or a relationship.

To have group members report ways they feel driven by the problem.

To have group members admit their hopelessness to manage the problem by themselves.

Spiritual awareness lead-in question:

Can you describe an event or situation that has caused you to think more about God in your search for help?

3. Spiritual Awareness: Romans 7:18–25; 8:1–2 (20–25 minutes)

The main objective of this session is to learn the aspects of how the apostle Paul dealt with powerlessness.

Aspects include:

• Paul recognized his own powerlessness (Rom. 7:18–20). In what way did Paul show an inability to do good?

How does Paul identify the sinful nature in his inability to do good in himself?

Do you see ways Paul may have been driven by the sinful nature?

• Paul recognized a war in his inner being (Rom. 7:21–24). How does Paul describe this war between good and evil?

How do you see his mind being affected?

In what ways can you identify with Paul being a prisoner in this war with his soul?

• Paul recognized that the only way to deal with his powerlessness was through Jesus Christ (Rom. 7:25–8:2). To whom did Paul express his thanks for his rescue from a wretched state?

How does he show that the road to God is through Jesus Christ?

Why do you think he addressed Jesus Christ as his Lord?

How did Paul express his freedom from condemnation?

Help group members understand the importance of admitting their powerlessness.

Assign Scripture references in Spiritual Awareness section to group members. The Scriptures should be read before the group and openly discussed as time permits. (Caution: Stay on the subject.)

4. Application (25 minutes)

Group discussion: Paul writes (2 Cor. 12:9–10), "But he [Jesus] said to me, 'My grace is sufficient for you, for my power is made perfect in weakness.' Therefore I will boast all the more gladly about my weaknesses, so that Christ's power may rest on me . . . For when I am weak, then I am strong."

In what ways can you apply these Scriptures to your personal struggle(s)?

Additional Scripture References:

Psalm 6:6–7; Psalm 31; Proverbs 28:26; Romans 3:9–10, 23; Romans 7 and 8

Session 2

Acknowledging My Belief in Jesus Christ

*Step 2 I now realize that my Creator, God
the Father, Son, and Holy Spirit, can
restore me to wholeness in Christ.*

1. Introduction (10–15 minutes)

Opening prayer
Use a "present tense go-around" (see p. 157)
Read **Step 2** to the group

2. Self-awareness (20–25 minutes)

The general goal of this session is to help group members acknowledge the need for a power greater than themselves. This higher power is Jesus Christ, the Son of God. It is likely that some participants have placed their trust in their self-will, false belief system, or their own ability to manage their lives. It is possible that some have had unpleasant experiences with Christians while others may have developed a poor concept of God. Others may see God as only for the weak or sick. Emphasize that there is hope for all in Christ. Be sensitive to the group members' comfort level since some may be dealing with anger toward God.

Specific goals for this session are:

To have group members report ways they have tried to manage their lives.

To have group members list the resources they have used to manage their lives.

To have group members discuss the feelings that come from trying to deal with a life-controlling problem within the sphere of their own strength.

Spiritual awareness lead-in question:

In what ways can wholeness in Christ help you deal with delusion?

3. Spiritual Awareness: Philippians 2:12–13 (20–25 minutes)

The main objective of this session is to learn the aspects of how God works in us to fulfill his purpose for our lives.

Aspects include:

• Paul encourages his friends to work out their "salvation with fear and trembling" (Phil. 2:12–13).

   What are some of the ways we can work out our salvation *as God works in us?*

   Why is it important to practice reverence *(fear and trembling)* for God?

- Paul emphasizes God's continuing work in us (Phil. 2:13). In what ways is God working in you?

What are some of the things you are doing *(continue to work out your salvation)* in response to God's work in you?

How do you view God's will and purpose in your life?

- Exercising faith in Jesus Christ is vital for salvation (Rom. 10:9–10).
What does it mean to you to confess with your mouth that Jesus is Lord?

What does it mean to you to "believe in your heart that God raised him [Jesus] from the dead?"

What is the result of confessing with your mouth that Jesus is Lord and believing in your heart that God raised Jesus from the dead?

Can you describe a time when it was difficult for you to place your trust in Christ?

- God—"an ever-present help in trouble" (Ps. 46:1). What comfort does this verse give you?

How do you picture God as your refuge?

Help group members understand that God works from the inside out (as he works in us we work out our salvation). See "Identifying Goals" on page 101.

Assign Scripture references in Spiritual Awareness section to group members. The Scriptures should be read before the group and openly discussed as time permits. (Caution: Stay on the subject.)

4. Application (25 minutes)

Group discussion: How would you describe your relationship with Jesus Christ?

Additional Scripture References:

Psalm 27:4–5; Psalm 34:18–22; Isaiah 12:2; Ezekiel 36:27; Mark 9:23–24; Mark 10:26–27; John 8:32; John 15:5; Romans 8:9; 2 Corinthians 1:9; Ephesians 3:20; Hebrews 11:6

IDENTIFYING GOALS		
Goals for My:	My Part	God's Part
Church		
Family		
Career		
Personal Needs		
Education		
Physical Needs		
	My Responsibility Continue to work out your salvation with fear and trembling (Phil. 2:12).	**God's Responsibility** For it is God who works in you to will and to act according to his good purpose (Phil. 2:13).

Session 3

Affirming My Need for the Care of God

*Step 3   I now make a conscious decision to
turn my entire will and life over to the
care and direction of Jesus Christ as
Teacher, Healer, Savior, and Lord.*

1. Introduction (10–15 minutes)

Opening prayer
Use a "present tense go-around" (see p. 157)
Read **Step 3** to the group

2. Self-awareness (20–25 minutes)

The general goal of this session is to help each group member
affirm his/her decision to turn his/her entire life over to God
through Jesus Christ. Emphasize that this step is commitment:
(1) Commitment to turn his/her will and life over to God, (2) A
decision is made to not be mastered by any substance, behavior
or personal relationship, (3) The control is turned over to the
care of God.

Specific goals for this session are:

To have group members report ways that they have resisted God's will for their lives.

To have group members report areas of denial in their lives that have led to obsessive and/or destructive behaviors.

To have group members discuss this decision to give up control of their lives.

Spiritual awareness lead-in question:

What areas of your life are the most difficult to turn over to the *care of God?*

3. Spiritual Awareness: Romans 12:1–2 (20–25 minutes)

The main objective of this session is to learn the aspects of surrendering our will and the direction of our lives to the care of God.

Aspects include:

• Having a merciful and compassionate God, we should present our bodies as living sacrifices as a "spiritual act of worship" (Rom. 12:1).

Why do you think Paul describes this as being holy and pleasing to God?

What does a living sacrifice mean to you?

- We are to guard against being conformed to the ways of this world (Rom. 12:2).
  In what ways have you felt pressure to conform to the "pattern of this world"?

- Our minds need renewal (Rom. 12:2).
  In what ways is the transformation of the mind a process?

- The Lord has a good and perfect will for everyone (Rom. 12:2).
  According to Paul we can test and approve God's will for our lives. What do you think he means?

- We are encouraged to trust in the Lord and acknowledge the Lord in all our ways (Prov. 3:5–6).
  In what ways have you depended "on your own understanding"?

How are you acknowledging the Lord for his direction in your life?

What do you expect from the Lord?

Help group members understand the significance of turning our lives over to the care of God.

Assign Scripture references in the Spiritual Awareness section to group members. The Scriptures should be read before the group and openly discussed as time permits. (Caution: Stay on the subject.)

4. Application (25 minutes)

Group discussion: A meaningful decision requires action on our part. What actions will accompany your decision to turn your life over to the *care of God?* How will you deal with the tendency to regain control of your life?

Additional Scripture References:

Joshua 1:8–9; Psalm 118:8–9; Proverbs 16:3; Isaiah 30:15; Isaiah 55:6–7; Jeremiah 29:11–14; Jeremiah 32:27; Mark 10:27; John 1:12–13; John 10:29–30; John 14:6; Galatians 2:20; Revelation 3:20

Session 4

Auditing My Life

Step 4 *Having made this decision, I now obey God's call in Scripture to make a fearless, ethical, moral, and scriptural inventory of my entire life in order to uncover all sins, mistakes, and character defects, and to make a written list of every item uncovered.*

1. Introduction (10–15 minutes)

Opening prayer
Use a "present tense go-around" (see p. 157)
Read **Step 4** to the group

2. Self-awareness (20–25 minutes)

Continue to emphasize the importance of steps 1–3, which are the building blocks for recovery. In this step an emphasis should be placed on personal inventory. Group members should be encouraged to search with honesty all aspects of their life without the use of excuses for their inappropriate behavior. As group members report their personal histories of life-controlling problems they should be reminded that God will guide their life. Remind the group members about the importance of doing their written list of thoughts (personal audit) assigned in the workbook. (See **Personal Audit** on p. 110.)

Specific goals for this session are:

To have group members list ways they have denied the reality of their condition.

To have group members describe ways they have blamed people, circumstances, situations, etc. for their condition.

To have group members discuss ways their behaviors have affected other people (family, friends, etc.).

Spiritual awareness lead-in question:

In what ways can a personal examination help you look to God for help?

3. Spiritual Awareness: Psalm 139:1–4, 23–24 (20–25 minutes)

The main objective of this session is to learn the aspects of how God encourages each of us to take a personal inventory of our life. Although experiencing the grieving process through repentance is healthy, emphasis should be placed on our new hope *in Christ.* It should be pointed out that Christ is our only hope as Savior, healer, and teacher. He will not disappoint us in our time of personal searching.

Aspects include:

- The Lord knows us personally (Ps. 139:1–2).
  What is your understanding of God knowing you on a personal basis?

  What do you think David means in verse 2, "You know when I sit and when I rise; you perceive my thoughts from afar"?

- The Lord knows our actions (Ps. 139:3–4).
  How does it make you feel knowing that God is aware of all our ways and even our words before they are spoken?

- David was open to personal examination (Ps. 139:23–24).
  How do you feel about God searching our hearts and testing our thoughts?

  In what ways can offensive motives deter God's leading in our lives?

- Restoration includes personal examination and testing (Lam. 3:40).
  Why is it important to "examine our ways and test them"?

- Jeremiah describes the heart as deceitful (Jer. 17:9–10). In what ways can a deceitful heart support our denial of a life-controlling problem?

Help group members understand that personal inventory before God is vital for recovery.

Assign Scripture references in Spiritual Awareness section to group members. The Scriptures should be read before the group and openly discussed as time permits. (Caution: Stay on the subject.)

4. Application (25 minutes)

Group discussion: King David was a man who failed God yet was willing to repent and conduct a personal inventory of his life. He is described as a man after God's own heart (Acts 13:22).

What lessons can we learn from David in conducting our personal inventory?

Additional Scripture References:

Jeremiah 23:24; Lamentations 3:19–23; John 6:68–69; John 14:26; John 16:13; Romans 8:26–27; 2 Corinthians 13:5–6; James 1:12

Personal Audit

My relationship with God:

My relationship with my family:

My relationship with my church:

My relationship with my friends:

Memory Verse

Search me, O God, and know my heart; test me and know my anxious thoughts (Ps. 139:23).

Session 5

Accounting for My Actions

Step 5 *After completing this inventory I now will to "walk in the light, as he is in the light" by admitting to myself, to God, and to at least one other person in Christ the exact nature of these wrongs.*

1. Introduction (10–15 minutes)

Opening prayer
Use an "affirmation go-around" (see p. 160)
Read **Step 5** to the group

2. Self-awareness (20–25 minutes)

The general goal of this session is to help group members admit to themselves, God, and others their thoughts prepared on paper in **Step 4**. Sharing with others helps remove the person from isolation caused by the wall of defenses used to protect himself/herself from more sorrow from the life-controlling problem(s). Emphasize the importance of sharing only those things that they feel comfortable in sharing with the other group members (remember to respect the comfort level of each group member). Although it may be helpful for the group members to share their concerns with another person who is *mature in Christ,* emphasize that only Christ can forgive sins. There may be some personal concerns that only *God needs to know.*

Specific goals for this session are:

To have group members report those items within their personal comfort level from their written list of wrongs prepared in **Step 4.**

To have group members discuss the isolation they have experienced due to a life-controlling problem.

To have group members discuss the type of person with whom they prefer to talk.

Spiritual awareness lead-in question:

Admitting the exact nature of my wrongs to myself and others is important. Why is it more important to admit our wrongs to God?

3. Spiritual Awareness: 1 John 1:5–10; 1 John 2:1–2 (20–25 minutes)

The main objective of this session is to learn the aspects of "walking in the light, as he is in the light."

Aspects include:

- God is light and truth (vv. 5–6).
  What does the term "in him there is no darkness at all" mean to you?

What hinders our fellowship with God?

- Walking in the light results in fellowship with God and one another (v. 7).
  How does walking in the light cleanse us from sin?

What is the significance of the blood of Jesus?

- John describes the cause and remedy for deceit (vv. 8–10). In what ways has deceit prevented us from being honest with ourselves?

Why is confession of sin necessary in our walk with God?

Why is denial of sin so destructive to our fellowship with God?

- Jesus is the mediator between God and man (1 John 2:1–2). What comfort and assurance do these verses give us?

- Confession and prayer are vital to the healing process (James 5:16).

Since Jesus is the forgiver of our sins, why is confession of faults to one another helpful?

Why is prayer so vital to our walking in the light?

Help group members understand the significance of turning our lives over to the care of God.

Assign Scripture references in Spiritual Awareness section to group members. The Scriptures should be read before the group and openly discussed as time permits. (Caution: Stay on the subject.)

4. Application (25 minutes)

Group discussion: Since our sins have been forgiven and nailed to the cross (Col. 2:13–15), our written list of wrongs (**Personal Audit**) should be destroyed in praise to our God. What is your prayer of thanksgiving?

Additional Scripture References:

Psalm 119:9–11; Proverbs 28:13; Jeremiah 14:20; Acts 2:37–38; Acts 3:19; Acts 13:38–39; Romans 3:23; Romans 14:12; Ephesians 5:13–14; 1 Timothy 1:15; Hebrews 9:14

Prayer List

Person and/or Situation   Request

Session 6

Agreeing with God

Step 6 *Having agreed with God about my sin-*
ful behavior, I now ask his forgiveness
through Christ and openly acknowl-
edge that I am forgiven according to
Scripture.

1. Introduction (10–15 minutes)

Opening prayer
Use an "affirmation go-around" (see p. 160)
Read **Step 6** to the group

2. Self-awareness (20–25 minutes)

In steps 1–5 emphasis has been placed on building a foundation for change. We have looked at our denial and delusion and
asked the Lord to give us clear thinking so we can follow him. In
this session, group members should be encouraged to continue
their denouncement of sin and focus on "walking out" the
changes in their lives.

Specific goals for this session are:

To have group members discuss the behaviors which have violated their value system.

To have group members discuss actions that they are taking to confront their negative trends of behavior.

To have group members discuss how negative trends of behavior have affected their self-esteem.

Spiritual awareness lead-in question:

What areas of self-management have been the most difficult for you to turn over to God?

3. Spiritual Awareness: Amos 3:3; James 4:7–10 (20–25 minutes)

The main objective of this session is to learn the aspects of how agreeing with God and walking with God go hand in hand.

Aspects include:

- Walking with God means harmony (Amos 3:3).
  Why is it difficult for two to walk together unless they are in agreement?

How do you see your change of behavior as a cooperative effort with the Lord?

- Walking with God means submission (James 4:7–8).
  What is the promise for those who resist the devil?

- Walking with God means humility (James 4:9–10).
  What is the promise for those who humble themselves "before the Lord"?

- Walking with God means that I agree with God that I am forgiven of my sins (Eph. 1:7).
  What does it mean to be freely forgiven of your sins?

What price did Christ pay for this forgiveness?

Help group members understand the importance of staying within God's boundaries in order to receive his blessings (see Jude 21 TLB).

Assign Scripture references in Spiritual Awareness section to group members. The Scriptures should be read before the group and openly discussed as time permits. (Caution: Stay on the subject.)

4. Application (25 minutes)

Group discussion: What outward changes in your life are happening as a result of your commitment to agree with God, allowing him to manage your life?

Additional Scripture References:

Psalm 27:13–14; Psalm 37:4–5; Psalm 118:17–18; Psalm 119:11; Proverbs 19:21; Proverbs 21:30–31; Isaiah 1:18–19; Romans 6:11–14; 2 Thessalonians 3:3; Hebrews 4:16; Jude 20–21

Session 7

Abandoning My Sins

Step 7 I now repent (turn away) from all these behaviors in thought, word, and deed, and ask God to remove each besetting sin, through Jesus Christ.

1. Introduction (10–15 minutes)

Opening prayer
Use an "affirmation go-around" (see p. 160)
Read **Step 7** to the group

2. Self-awareness (20–25 minutes)

In this session group members should be encouraged to continue their emphasis on "walking out" the changes in their life. To do this there must be a focus on "turning from" our sins. These shortcomings should be approached with an attitude of surrender. Having confessed them to Christ and others, now is the time to allow him to purify us.

Specific goals for this session are:

To have group members report their experiences of "walking out" the changes since the previous meeting.

To have group members discuss character defects that they continue to struggle with.

To have group members report any struggles that they may be experiencing from turning over surrender of their lives to God's care.

Spiritual awareness lead-in question:

What is your definition of repentance?

3. Spiritual Awareness: Hebrews 12:1–3 (20–25 minutes)

The main objective of this session is to learn the aspects of repentance (turning away from) of behaviors that are destructive to God's plan for our life.

Aspects include:

- We are encouraged to deal with "everything that hinders" us (v. 1).

  Why do you think the writer of Hebrews refers to "a great cloud of witnesses"? What relationship is there to the preceding chapter?

In what ways can we become entangled with certain sins?

What does "run the race with perseverance" mean to you? In what ways is the Christian life a race?

• We are encouraged to focus our attention on Jesus (v. 2). How do you picture Jesus as the source of your faith? How do you picture Jesus as the finisher of your faith?

In view of verse 2, what does it mean to you that Jesus "endured the cross"?

• We are encouraged to consider the endurance of Jesus (v. 3). Jesus received opposition.
What are some ways God is helping you overcome opposition from destructive behaviors?

What comfort do you receive from the encouragement to "not grow weary"?

• Repentance is proved by one's deeds (Acts 26:20).
List examples of actions that are changing based on your "turning to God."

- Repentance brings a refreshing from the Lord (Acts 3:19). Describe this verse in your own words.

Help group members understand the value of repentance and faith in Christ.

Assign Scripture references in Spiritual Awareness section to group members. The Scriptures should be read before the group and openly discussed as time permits. (Caution: Stay on the subject.)

4. Application (25 minutes)

Group discussion: Solomon writes (Prov. 3:5–6), "Trust in the LORD with all your heart and lean not on your own understanding; in all your ways acknowledge him, and he will make your paths straight."

How do you plan to apply these verses to your life when dealing with hindrances to your walk in Christ?

Additional Scripture References:

Job 11:13–19; Psalm 51:10; Psalm 90:8; Psalm 103:2–3; Ezekiel 18:30–32; Daniel 4:27; John 5:14; John 8:10–11; Acts 20:21; Romans 5 and 6; Romans 12:1–2; 2 Corinthians 2:10; 2 Corinthians 10:5; Philippians 4:6; Colossians 3:17; 1 Peter 5:6–7; 1 John 2:3–6

Session 8

Amending My Ways

Step 8 *I now make a list of all persons I have harmed in thought, word, and deed, and a list of all persons I believe have harmed me, and will to make amends to all of them.*

1. Introduction (10–15 minutes)

Opening prayer
Use an "affirmation go-around" (see p. 160)
Read **Step 8** to the group

2. Self-awareness (20–25 minutes)

As the Lord helps us become aware of the delusion in our lives we are faced with the reality that others may have been harmed by our behaviors. Emphasize that continued cover-up or blaming others for our behaviors can result in further delusion and bitterness. Forgiving ourselves and others through Christ helps us overcome the past.

Specific goals for this session are:

To encourage group members to make an amends list (if they have not completed their assignment in the workbook). See page 128.

To have group members discuss relationships that need to be amended.

To have group members discuss ways they have tried to cover up for their behaviors.

To have group members discuss past misdeeds that they cannot correct and have turned over to God.

Spiritual awareness lead-in question:

How does making amends through Christ help free you from the past?

3. Spiritual Awareness: 2 Corinthians 5:17–21 (20–25 minutes)

The main objective of this session is to learn the aspects of the ministry of reconciliation.

Aspects include:

- Being *in Christ* helps us deal with the past (v. 17).
  What does being "a new creation" mean to you?

How does "the old has gone, the new has come" apply to your life?

- Reconciliation comes through Christ (v. 18).
  What does reconciliation *through Christ* mean to you?

  How do you view "the ministry of reconciliation"?

- Our sins are not held against us (v. 19).
  How does it make you feel knowing that the sins of the past have been forgiven?

  How do you feel about God committing to you "the message of reconciliation"? How do you express this in view of broken relationships?

- We are ambassadors for Christ (v. 20).
  What is your view of an ambassador of Christ?

  Why do you think Paul focuses on Christ as the key to reconciliation with God?

- Our identity is *in Christ* (v. 21).
  How do you picture the sinless Christ becoming sin for us?

What does it mean to you that in Christ we "become the righteousness of God"?

Help group members understand the importance of forgiving themselves and others (Matt. 6:14–15; Matt. 18:21–35; Col. 3:13).

Assign Scripture references in Spiritual Awareness section to group members. The Scriptures should be read before the group and openly discussed as time permits. (Caution: Stay on the subject.)

4. Application (25 minutes)

Group discussion: In view of Jesus' statement, "Do to others as you would have them do to you" (Luke 6:31), how do you plan your approach in amending broken or strained relationships?

Additional Scripture References:

Leviticus 19:17–18; Psalm 19:13–14; Psalm 32:1–2; Hosea 11:1–4; Matthew 5:9, 43–45; Mark 12:31; Luke 6:31; Ephesians 4:29–32; 1 John 4:7–12

Amends

Person   Relationship   Actions to Correct

Acting on My Amends

Step 9 *I now go directly to these persons to forgive and to seek forgiveness, reconciliation, restitution, or release whenever and with whomever possible, unless to do so would cause further harm.*

1. Introduction (10–15 minutes)

Opening prayer
Use an "accountability go-around" (see p. 160)
Read **Step 9** to the group

2. Self-awareness (20–25 minutes)

The general goal of this session is to assist group members in going directly to those who may have been harmed by strained or broken relationships. Emphasize the importance of using wisdom in seeking forgiveness and reconciliation. Approach only those with whom you have access and would not cause further harm (further harm includes areas that may cause damage which would be beyond repair). Remind group members that the purpose is to reconcile, not to document the other person's mistakes or to blame others.

Specific goals for this session are:

To have group members discuss strained or broken relationships with people with whom they have accessibility and making amends would not cause further harm.

To have group members discuss former harmful relationships with people who are no longer approachable (because the person is deceased, or because of concern for further harm).

To have group members discuss how they are turning their inaccessible, strained, or broken relationships which cannot be further dealt with over to God.

Spiritual awareness lead-in question:

Describe your present feelings about your peace with God.

3. Spiritual Awareness: Matthew 5:23–24; Luke 15:18–24 (20–25 minutes)

The main objective of this session is to learn the aspects of making restitution and/or releasing to the Lord those relationships which cannot be restored because of inaccessibility or likelihood of further harm.

Aspects include:

- We are encouraged to make peace with our brother (vv. 23–24).

  Describe these verses in your own words.

In your times of prayer and meditation have you been reminded of strained and broken relationships? Describe them.

In what ways can you apply these verses to your strained or broken relationships?

- The prodigal son made peace with his father and heaven (Luke 15:18–21).
  What action did this son take to make peace with his father and heaven?

Why was it important for him to admit his sin against his father and heaven?

How do you picture the son's humility?

Describe the reconciliation of the father and son in your own words.

Help group members understand the importance of taking responsibility for their own actions wherever possible. Comfort them with the assurance that God helps us with those broken relationships that are beyond our control (1 Peter 5:7).

Assign Scripture references in Spiritual Awareness section to group members. The Scriptures should be read before the group and openly discussed as time permits. (Caution: Stay on the subject.)

4. Application (25 minutes)

Group discussion: Describe difficult situations that you might face in your effort to make amends. In what ways can this group help you? In what ways can you help support others in this group?

Additional Scripture References:

Numbers 5:5–7; Isaiah 1:18–20; Ezekiel 33:15–16; Luke 6:35; Romans 12:17–18; Ephesians 5:21; Philippians 2:3–4; 1 Thessalonians 5:11

Session 10

Analyzing My Walk with Christ

*Step 10 I now consciously and prayerfully
continue to "walk in the light" by
unceasingly taking personal inventory
of all my temptations and sins, and by
keeping a constantly open relationship
with God, myself, and other persons.*

1. Introduction (10–15 minutes)

Opening prayer
Use an "accountability go-around" (see p. 160)
Read **Step 10** to the group

2. Self-awareness (20–25 minutes)

In this session emphasis should be focused on the group members maintaining the gains they have made to this point. It is helpful for group members to discuss their victories but also be aware of their weaknesses to relapse into their former life-style.

Specific goals for this session are:

To have group members discuss the gains that they have made to remain free of life-controlling problems.

To have group members discuss triggering devices that can lead to relapse. Triggering devices include:

Socializing with former friends that have a bad influence.

Withdrawal from church services and support group.

"Talking the talk" but not "walking the walk."

Going to places that have negative influence.

Avoiding those who are concerned friends.

Spiritual awareness lead-in question:

What does an open relationship with God mean to you?

3. Spiritual Awareness: 1 Corinthians 10:12–13; 2 Corinthians 3:4–6 (20–25 minutes)

The main objective of this session is to learn the aspects of being confident in Christ (not our own accomplishments) and of being open before the Lord about the temptations which can hinder our walk with Christ.

Aspects include:

• Paul warns against being overconfident (v. 12).
  Why do you think Paul warns us about falling?

  How do you relate to this verse?

- Paul shows how to deal with temptation (v. 13).
  Why is your temptation not unique?

Describe God's part in helping you with temptation.

Describe your responsibility in dealing with temptation.

- Our confidence should be in Christ, not in our own
  resources (2 Cor. 3:4–6).
  In what ways can you apply these verses to your life?

How do you think God makes us "competent as ministers"?

- God does not tempt us (James 1:13–15).
  In view of these verses describe what can happen if you give
  in to temptation.

Help group members understand that an open relationship
with God is the key to dealing with overconfidence and
temptations.

Assign Scripture references in Spiritual Awareness section to
group members. The Scriptures should be read before the group
and openly discussed as time permits. (Caution: Stay on the
subject.)

4. Application (25 minutes)

Group discussion: Describe your progress at this point.

Additional Scripture References:

Psalm 4:3–5; Psalm 34:12–14; Psalm 55:22; Psalm 139:1–4; Proverbs 30:8–9; Matthew 26:41; Galatians 6:4–5; Ephesians 4:25–26; James 1:23–25

Session 11

Anchoring My Walk with Christ

Step 11 I now continue in regular Scripture study, prayer, worship, and fellowship to increase God's will in my life.

1. Introduction (10–15 minutes)

Opening prayer
Use an "accountability go-around" (see p. 160)
Read **Step 11** to the group

2. Self-awareness (20–25 minutes)

This session is a continuation of Session 10. Turning our lives over to the care of God and dealing with our character defects is important. However, now the challenge is to continue to walk out these changes. Focus on the need for regular times of prayer and meditation which will help direct our thoughts on God and his will for our lives.

Specific goals for this session are:

To have group members discuss how they are dealing with negative thoughts.

To have group members discuss why it is important not to permit negative thoughts to linger in our minds.

To have group members discuss their personal need to meditate on God and his Word.

Spiritual awareness lead-in question:

In what ways is God influencing your daily inventory of thoughts and actions?

3. Spiritual Awareness: Colossians 3:12–17 (20–25 minutes)

The main objective of this session is to learn the aspects of God directing our lives on a daily basis through prayer, study, and meditation of his Word.

Aspects include:

• As God's chosen people we are to clothe ourselves with his garments (v. 12).
As God's representatives, in what ways are we to clothe ourselves? Describe each one in your own words.

• Paul emphasizes forgiveness (v. 13).

What does "bear with each other" mean to you? Who is our example for forgiveness? Describe what Christ's example of forgiveness means to you.

• Love and perfect unity go hand in hand (v. 14).
  What does "put on love" mean to you? What part does love play in bringing unity among believers?

• The "peace of Christ" plays an important role in directing our lives (v. 15).
  What role does the "peace of Christ" play? Why do you think Paul encourages us to be thankful? How can you apply this verse to your life?

• We are encouraged to "let the word of Christ dwell in us" (v. 16).
  In what ways do you picture the "word of Christ" being the foundation of Christian activities listed in this verse?

  Why do you think Paul emphasizes "gratitude in your hearts to God"?

• We are encouraged to do all "in the name of the Lord Jesus" (v. 17).
  How can you apply this verse to your life?

Help group members understand the importance of daily fellowship with God.

Assign Scripture references in Spiritual Awareness section to group members. The Scriptures should be read before the group and openly discussed as time permits. (Caution: Stay on the subject.)

4. Application (25 minutes)

Group discussion: Describe your present schedule for your personal devotions. How do you feel about your persistence? How do you deal with interruptions?

Additional Scripture References:

Joshua 1:8; 1 Kings 8:56–61; Psalm 1:1–3; Psalm 19:14; Psalm 25:1–5; Psalm 63:1–7; Psalm 89:15; Isaiah 30:21; Matthew 6:33–34; Matthew 7:7; Mark 11:24; Mark 12:28–33; Acts 2:42; Philippians 4:6–9

Session 12

Advancing My Faith in Christ

Step 12 Recognizing the impact of God in my life, I now intentionally share these principles and their effect with others as God's Spirit leads, and will to practice these principles in all areas of my life.

1. Introduction (10–15 minutes)

Opening prayer
Use an "accountability go-around" (see p. 160)
Read **Step 12** to the group

2. Self-awareness (20–25 minutes)

This session brings us to a point of completion; however, our spiritual walk with Christ is not complete. As group members continue to walk out the truths learned and applied in this course, the focus should be placed on reaching out to others who need our help. The general goal of this session is to encourage group members to share with others the principles they have learned. As they share with others what the Lord has done in their lives, their confidence will be enhanced.

Specific goals for this session are:

To have group members share reasons they feel a responsibility to share with others.

To have group members discuss ways they feel free to share with others since God has helped them with their stronghold.

To have group members discuss any anxiety they may have about sharing with others.

Spiritual awareness lead-in question:

Describe a significant person(s) God used in helping you. In what ways did this person(s) help you?

3. Spiritual Awareness: 1 Peter 3:15–18 (20–25 minutes)

The main objective of this session is to learn the aspects of sharing our faith in Christ and our comfort received from God with others.

Aspects include:

• Christ should have a special place in our hearts (v. 15).
What do you think Peter means by "in your hearts set apart Christ as Lord"?

According to this verse we should be prepared "to give the reason for the hope" we have. When should we be prepared? What is our hope based on?

Why do you think Peter encourages us to share our hope "with gentleness and respect"? Give examples of ways we can share "with gentleness and respect."

- We are to maintain "a clear conscience" (v. 16).
  Sharing our faith with gentleness and respect along with a clear conscience is important. In view of this verse, why is it important?

- God's will for our lives may include suffering (v. 17).
  Can you think of ways you have suffered for doing good? For doing evil? What is the difference between suffering for good and evil?

- Christ died for our sins (v. 18).
  Describe in your own words the significance of "Christ died for our sins once for all."

In view of this verse, why did he die for our sins?

How was he made alive?

- We are to help those being led to the way of death (Prov. 24:11; Jude 22–25).

Help group members understand the need to share with others their faith in Christ. By doing so group members will experience an enrichment from Christ.

Assign Scripture references in Spiritual Awareness section to group members. The Scriptures should be read before the group and openly discussed as time permits. (Caution: Stay on the subject.)

4. Application (25 minutes)

Group discussion: Paul writes (2 Cor. 1:3–4), "Praise be to the God and Father of our Lord Jesus Christ, the Father of compassion and the God of all comfort, who comforts us in all our troubles, so that we can comfort those in any trouble with the comfort we ourselves have received from God."

What is your plan to comfort others "with the comfort we ourselves have received from God"? Why do you think it is important to share the comfort we have received from the Lord? How will you depend on the Holy Spirit to guide you?

Additional Scripture References:

Psalm 40:8–10; Isaiah 61:1–3; Jeremiah 20:9; Micah 6:8; Matthew 28:19–20; Mark 5:19; Luke 4:18–19; 2 Corinthians 3:17–18; Galatians 5:1; Galatians 6:1–5; Ephesians 5:8–10; Ephesians 6:10–18; Colossians 4:5–6; Revelation 12:11

Part Three
Resources

Selected Scriptures

Anger	Prov. 14:29; 15:18; 16:32; 17:27; 19:11; 29:11; Eccles. 7:9; Matt. 5:22–26; Phil. 2:3–4; James 1:19–21; Eph. 4:26–27
Anxiety/Worry	Ps. 43:5; Matt. 6:31–32; Luke 12:29–31; 1 Peter 5:7
Bereavement/Loss	Deut. 31:8; Pss. 27:10; 119:50; Lam. 3:32–33; 2 Cor. 6:10; Phil. 3:8
Fatherless	Ps. 68:5
Bitterness (General)	Eph. 4:31–32; Heb. 12:15; 1 John 2:11
Won't listen	Prov. 15:32
Malice	Col. 3:8; Eph. 4:31; 1 Peter 2:1
Resentments	1 Peter 2:1–3; 1 John 2:11; Prov. 26:23–26
Revenge	Rom. 12:19
Slander	Eph. 4:31; 1 Peter 2:1; Ps. 69
Unforgiveness	Matt. 6:14–15; Mark 11:25–26; Eph. 4:32; 2 Cor. 2:10–11; Matt. 18:21–22
Comfort	Gen. 18:25; Rom. 8:26–28; 15:4; 2 Cor. 1:3–5; 2 Thess. 2:16–17; Heb. 13:5
Complaining	1 Cor. 10:10; Phil. 2:14; 1 Peter 4:9
Condemnation	Ezek. 18:20; Ps. 34:22; Rom. 4:5; 8:1; 1 John 1:7; 3:19–21
Confidence (in God)	Gen. 18:25; Isa. 30:15; Jer. 9:24; 32:17–19, 27; Ps. 138:3; Prov. 3:26; 14:26; Rom. 8:26–28; 2 Cor. 2:14; Eph. 3:11–12; Phil. 4:13; Heb. 10:35
Contentment	Phil. 4:11–12; 1 Tim. 6:6–10; Heb. 13:5–6
Danger	Ps. 34:17, 19; Isa. 43:2; Rom. 14:8; James 4:7
Depression	1 Kings 19:5; Ps. 27:14; Isa. 60:1; John 16:33; 2 Cor. 4:1–17; Gal. 6:9–10; Phil. 4:8–13; 2 Thess. 3:11–13; Heb. 12:4–7

Disappointment in God	Gen. 18:25; Pss. 43:5; 55:22; 126:6; Jer. 9:24
Discouragement	1 Sam. 30:6; Ps. 27:14; John 14:27; 16:33; Acts 14:22; Rom. 5:5; 15:13; 2 Cor. 10:5; Eph. 6:16; 1 Thess. 5:11; Heb. 2:3–13; 10:24–25
In ministry	1 Cor. 15:58; Gal. 6:9
Divorce	Mal. 2:14–16; Matt. 5:31–32; 19:4–6; Mark 10:11–12; Luke 16:18; 1 Cor. 7:10–11, 27
Drunkenness	Rom. 14:21; 1 Cor. 6:9–11; 10:31–32; Eph. 5:18; 1 Tim. 3:8; 1 Peter 4:3
Envy/Jealousy	Prov. 23:17; 1 Cor. 13:4; Gal. 5:26; Heb. 13:5; James 3:14–16
Faith	Acts 13:39; 15:8–11; Rom. 4:3–5; 10:11, 17; Gal. 2:16; Phil. 4:13, 19; Heb. 12:2; James 1:3; 1 Peter 1:7
Fear (General)	Pss. 27:1; 34:4; 56:3, 11; John 14:27; Rom. 8:31; 2 Tim. 1:7
Cowardice	1 Sam. 17:24; Prov. 28:1
Depression	1 Kings 19:3–4; John 4:8
Doubts	Matt. 21:21; Rom. 14:23
Indecisions	James 1:5–8
Inferiority	Job 13:2
Of death	Ps. 116:15; Rom. 14:8; Phil. 1:21; 1 Thess. 5:9–10
Of Satan	Luke 10:19; Rom. 8:38–39; James 4:7
Pride	Prov. 16:18
Superstition	Prov. 28:1; Mark 6:14–16
Timidity	2 Tim. 1:7
Forgiveness	Pss. 32:5; 103:3; Prov. 28:13; Isa. 55:7; John 5:24; 6:47; Acts 10:43; 13:39; 26:18; Heb. 8:12; James 5:15–16; 1 John 1:9
Forgiving	Matt. 6:14–15; Mark 11:25; Eph. 4:32; Col. 3:13
Freedom	Rom. 6:6–7, 11–14; Rev. 1:5
Friendships	Prov. 14:7; 18:24; Rom. 12:16; 1 Cor. 15:33; 2 Cor. 6:14; 2 Tim. 2:21; James 4:4
Gospel	Acts 2:22–24; 10:38–43; 13:30–39; 1 Cor. 15:3–4; Titus 3:5; 1 Peter 2:22–24

Greed	Prov. 28:22; Matt. 6:19–24; Eph. 5:5; Col. 3:5; 1 Tim. 6:5–10
Guidance	Ps. 32:8; Isa. 30:21; 58:11; John 16:7, 13; Rom. 8:14
Hatred	1 John 2:9–11; 4:19–21
Help	Pss. 34:7; 37:5, 24; 55:22; Isa. 54:17; Jer. 29:11–13; 2 Cor. 2:14; 9:8; Heb. 4:16; 1 Peter 5:7
Homosexuality	Lev. 18:22; 20:13; Rom. 1:24, 27, 32; 1 Cor. 6:9–11
Inspiration of Word	Jer. 8:9; Matt. 5:17–18; 22:43; 1 Thess. 2:13; 2 Tim. 3:16–17; Heb. 4:12; 2 Peter 1:19–21; 3:16
Intolerance	
Bigotry	Rom. 15:7; Gal. 3:28; Col. 3:11
Criticism	Num. 11:1; James 5:9
Gossip	1 Tim. 5:13
Hatred	1 John 4:19–21
Jealousy	Rom. 13:13; 1 Cor. 3:3; 13:4; Gal. 5:20–21; James 3:14–16
Judgmental Spirit	Matt. 7:1–2; Rom. 14:10
Rebellion	Num. 16:1–11
Revenge	Rom. 12:19
Snobbery	Rom. 12:16; 15:7; Phil. 2:3
Judging	Matt. 7:1; Rom. 14:10; 1 Cor. 4:3–5; James 5:9
Laziness	Prov. 15:19; Rom. 12:11; Eph. 4:28; Col. 3:23; 1 Thess. 4:11–12; 2 Thess. 3:10–12; Titus 1:12–13
Love (God's)	Jer. 31:3; John 3:16; 15:9; Rom. 5:8; 8:38–39; 1 John 3:1; 4:10–11
Masturbation	Matt. 5:28; Rom. 13:14; 2 Cor. 10:5; 1 Thess. 4:3–5
Moral Impurity	Rom. 13:13–14; 1 Cor. 6:9–11; Eph. 5:5; Col. 3:5–6; 1 Thess. 4:4–8; 2 Tim. 2:22; Titus 2:12–15; Heb. 13:4
Perseverance	1 Cor. 13:7; Phil. 1:6; 1 Thess. 5:24; 2 Tim. 1:12; 2:12–13; Heb. 4:16; 10:35–12:1; James 5:11
Pride	Prov. 16:18; Jer. 9:23–24; Rom. 12:16; 1 Cor. 1:26–29; Gal. 5:26; 6:3, 14
Procrastination	Rom. 12:11; Eph. 5:15–16
Quarrelsome	Rom. 14:19; Gal. 5:15; 2 Tim. 2:24–25; Heb. 12:14; James 4:1–2

Rebellion	1 Sam. 15:22–23; Jer. 5:3; Rom. 13:2, 5; 1 Tim. 1:9; Titus 1:6; Heb. 13:17; 1 Peter 2:13–15; 4:7
Rejection	Isa. 53:3–4; Luke 6:22; Heb. 13:5
Repentance	Acts 3:19–21; Rom. 3:21–26; 2 Cor. 7:9–10; 2 Tim. 2:25; 26:18–20
Righteousness	Jer. 23:5–6; Rom. 3:21–26; 4:3, 13, 22; Gal. 2:21; 3:6; Phil. 3:9–10; 1 Tim. 6:11; Titus 2:11–12; 1 John 3:10
Self-ambition	Rom. 2:8; Phil. 1:17; James 3:16
Self-control	Ps. 119:11; Prov. 25:28; Luke 22:40; Rom. 12:2; 2 Cor. 10:5; Gal. 5:22–24; Phil. 4:8–9; 1 Thess. 4:11–12; 2 Thess. 3:10–12
Self-dignity (in Christ)	Gal. 2:19–20; 3:26, 29; Eph. 5:8; 1 Peter 2:5, 9; 1 John 2:12–14; 3:2, 19
Self-indulgence	Prov. 21:17; Matt. 23:25; Titus 1:6
Self-pity	James 1:21–25
Self-willed	1 Cor. 10:33; Titus 1:7; 2 Peter 2:10
Selfishness	Rom. 13:8–10; 1 Cor. 10:33–11:1; Phil. 2:3
Sickness	Ps. 103:3; Isa. 53:4; Matt. 8:17; James 5:15–16; 1 Peter 2:24
Sin Cycle	Judges 2:10–23; Neh. 9:26–31; Ps. 106:6–48; 1 Cor. 10:1–13
Spiritual Growth	2 Cor. 1:12; Gal. 5:24–25; 6:1–2; Eph. 3:17–19; 6:10–18; Col. 1:9–11; 3:16; 2 Tim. 2:15; 2 Peter 1:5–8; 3:18
Strength	Pss. 27:14; 28:7; 138:3; Isa. 41:10; 49:29, 31; 2 Cor. 9:8; 12:9; Phil. 4:13; 1 Thess. 3:2–3
Suffering (Sin)	Ps. 34:19; Jer. 2:19; 5:25; John 16:33; Acts 14:22; Rom. 8:18; Gal. 6:7; Phil. 3:9–10; 1 Thess. 3:3; 2 Tim. 1:12;
(for God)	1 Peter 2:11; 2:20–23; 4:12–13, 16, 19; 5:9–10
Testing/Trial	Prov. 17:3; 1 Cor. 10:12–13; James 1:2–4, 12; 1 Peter 1:6–7; 4:12–13; 5:9–10; Jude 24
Thankfulness	Eph. 5:20; Phil. 4:6; Col. 3:17; 1 Thess. 5:18
Trust	Pss. 5:11; 18:2; 37; 118:8–9

Phases of Life-controlling Problems

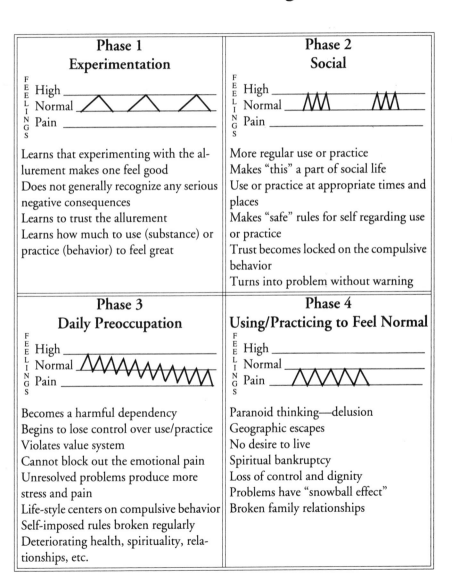

Phase 1
Experimentation

FEELINGS High / Normal / Pain

Learns that experimenting with the allurement makes one feel good

Does not generally recognize any serious negative consequences

Learns to trust the allurement

Learns how much to use (substance) or practice (behavior) to feel great

Phase 2
Social

FEELINGS High / Normal / Pain

More regular use or practice

Makes "this" a part of social life

Use or practice at appropriate times and places

Makes "safe" rules for self regarding use or practice

Trust becomes locked on the compulsive behavior

Turns into problem without warning

Phase 3
Daily Preoccupation

FEELINGS High / Normal / Pain

Becomes a harmful dependency

Begins to lose control over use/practice

Violates value system

Cannot block out the emotional pain

Unresolved problems produce more stress and pain

Life-style centers on compulsive behavior

Self-imposed rules broken regularly

Deteriorating health, spirituality, relationships, etc.

Phase 4
Using/Practicing to Feel Normal

FEELINGS High / Normal / Pain

Paranoid thinking—delusion

Geographic escapes

No desire to live

Spiritual bankruptcy

Loss of control and dignity

Problems have "snowball effect"

Broken family relationships

Communication by Care-fronting

Definitions

Caring

A good word.

Confronting

A word with bad connotations because it's often done when angry.

Care-fronting

A good word because it is confronting in a caring way. Caring is the first word. Therefore, the caring must be genuine. The confronting is not negative because it is done out of love.

Care-fronting is a way to communicate with love and truth, with both impact and respect.

Five Options of Dealing with Conflict

I'll get him

"I win, you lose, because I am right and you're wrong." This is all power and little or no love.

I'll get out

"I'm uncomfortable, so I'll withdraw from the conflict." "The situation is hopeless because people cannot be changed." A way of avoiding conflict can be advantageous for instant safety. There is no risk of power and no trusting love.

I'll give in

"I'll yield to be nice since I need your friendship." "I will be nice and submit to your demands so that we can be friends." You become a doormat who is frustrated and smiling.

I'll meet you halfway

"I have only half of the truth and I need your half." The attitude of creative compromise. Compromise is a gift to human relationships, and conflict is natural. Compromise is the willingness to give a little to work out a satisfactory solution for everyone. The danger of compromise is the risk that my half-truth and your half-truth may not give the total truth. You may have two half-truths, or it may produce a whole untruth. You must care enough to tussle with truth so it can be tested, retested, refined, and perhaps you'll find more of it through working together.

I care enough to confront

"I want a relationship and I also want honest integrity." Conflict is viewed as neutral (neither good nor bad) and natural (neither to be avoided nor short-circuited). This is an "I care" and "I want" position. This says, "I want to stay in a respectful relationship with you, and I want you to know where I stand and what I am feeling, needing, valuing, and wanting."

Caring and Confronting

I care about our relationship	and	I feel deeply about this issue.
I want to hear your view	and	I want to clearly express my view.
I want to respect your insights	and	I want respect for mine.
I give you my loving, honest respect	and	I want your caring-confronting response.

Care-fronting invites another to change but does not demand it.

Ways of Care-fronting without Being Judgmental

Focus your feedback on the action, not on the actor.

This gives the person the freedom to change his behavior without feeling personal rejection. **Example:** "When someone criticizes people who are not present, as you were doing a moment ago, I get uptight. I'd encourage you to say what you have to say to the person."

Focus your feedback on your observations, not on your conclusions.

Comment not on what you think, imagine, or infer, but on what you have actually seen or heard. Conclusions will evoke immediate defensiveness. **Example:** "You are not looking at me and not answering when I speak. Please give me both attention and answer."

Focus your feedback on descriptions, not on judgments.

Do not comment on another's behavior as nice or rude, right or wrong. Use a clear, accurate description in neutral language. When a value judgment is received there is a momentary break in contact. **Example:** "I am aware that your reply to my request for information was silence. Please tell me what this means."

Focus feedback on quantity, not on quality.

Comment not on character trait or classification (qualities) of the other person, but on the amount of feeling, expression or action (quantity). Use adverbs (which tell how much) rather than adjectives (which tell what kind of). Use terms denoting more or less (quantity) rather than either/or categories (quality). **Example:** "You talk considerably more than others," not "You were a loudmouth." "You have asked for and received more of my time than any other student," not "you are clinging, dependent, and always demanding my time."

Focus feedback on ideas, information, and alternatives, not on advice and answers.

Comment not with instructions on what to do with the data you have to offer, but with the data, the facts, the additional options. The more options available, the less likely is a premature solution. **Example:** "I've several other options that you may have thought about, but let me run them by you again."

Focus feedback, not on why, but on what and how.

"Why" critiques values, motives and intents. "Why" is judgmental. "What" and "how" relate to observable actions, behaviors, words and tone of voice. **Example:** "Here is where we are, let's examine it."

Care-fronting focuses on action, observations, descriptions, quantity, information, alternatives, and dealing with what and how in the here and now. It does not focus on actor, conclusions, judgments, qualities, advice or why.

When you are care-fronting, it should be done caringly, gently, constructively, and clearly. Never care-front with any possible interpretations of blaming, shaming or punishing.

Reprinted by permission from the book *Caring Enough to Confront* by David Augsburger, copyright by Herald Press, Scottdale, PA 15683.

Sharing Questions

A very good tool to help build relationships in a Bible study group is to use a sharing question at each group meeting. These are one or two sentence questions which invite people to tell the group something about themselves. It gives people permission to talk about themselves in a structured context where all share something and all listen to the others. These are not questions which ask for knowledge, information or opinions about issues, but questions which encourage people to talk about themselves—their past experiences, present situations, hopes for the future, joys and sorrows, struggles and successes. The thrust is not on sharing ideas or concepts but on sharing ourselves. The sharing question is used to help members to move beyond chit-chat and shallow conversation to tell something about themselves to help other members of the group get to know them.

Past Tense Sharing Questions

These questions ask people to share something about their personal history.

Examples

Where did you live when you were twelve years old, and what is one strong memory you have from that time?

Who was the most influential person in your childhood, and why?

What was the most memorable holiday you ever took, and why?

When, if ever, did God become more than a word to you, and how did that happen?

What is one experience of success that you can remember, and what did it mean to you?

What is one quality from your parents that you wanted to keep, and anything you wished you could change?

When was the first time you heard about Jesus, and what did you think about him?

When did you meet your spouse, and what do you remember from that time?

What were the Christmas holidays like for you when you were growing up, and how did you feel about them?

What has been your most important spiritual experience?

What was your relationship to a church as you grew up, and how did you feel about it?

What was the most exciting (challenging, difficult, growth-producing, enjoyable, or terrible) part of your life up to now, and why?

These past tense questions are especially appropriate in the early stages of a new group and when new members join. By inviting people to share their pasts, we begin to know something about the influences and experiences that have helped to make them who they are.

Present Tense Sharing Questions

These questions invite people to discuss what is happening in their lives at the present time. The very recent past may be a part of these questions, but the focus is on the experiences and feelings that are part of daily life now.

Examples

What do you do on a typical Tuesday? When do you get up, what do you do during the day, and when do you go to bed?

What is one part of your life that you enjoy, and one part that is difficult for you?

What is your favorite spot in your home or garden, and why?

What is a good thing happening in your life right now, and what makes it good?

What do you like to do for fun?

When you have some free time to yourself, what do you like to do?

What is one thing that you worried about or struggled with this past week?

What are you looking forward to, and what are you reluctant to face, during the next week?

What is one decision facing you that you find difficult, and why?

What is a satisfying relationship and/or a frustrating relationship in your life, and what makes it so?

When do you struggle with yourself and win, or when do you struggle with yourself and lose? How do you feel about that?

What is the most important, most meaningful or most satisfying thing that you do in a week, and why?

What is one thing that gave you joy or a sense of accomplishment this week?

What is one thing you are proud of about yourself?

What is one thing at which you are good, and one thing at which you are bad?

Where are you changing or growing in your life, and what helps and what hinders that process?

What spiritual discipline do you find the easiest or the most difficult?

What do you like about your job, and is there anything you find boring?

Present tense questions help us to talk about what is going on in our lives right now. Often group members do not know what fellow members do in their daily lives or how they feel about what is happening to them unless such questions are asked.

Future Tense Sharing Questions

These questions focus on what is ahead, usually not in the near future but a little further off. They help people to talk about their desires for change, their hopes, dreams, expectations and possibilities. Questions of this type are usually asked after a group has been together for a while.

Examples

If you knew you could not fail, and money was no problem, what one thing would you like to do in the next five years?

If you could change one thing about yourself or develop one quality that you do not have, what would it be?

What is one relationship you would like to strengthen, and what steps could you take to develop it?

What would be the perfect holiday for you? Where would it be, and what would you do?

If you could change one thing about the world, what would it be, and why?

If you could accomplish one positive change for good in your church, what would it be? How might you go about it?

If you went home and found a check written to you for one million dollars, how would you spend the money?

What would you like to have said about you at your funeral?

How do you want your children to remember you, and what are you doing to ensure those memories?

What is one dream or hope you have for the future?

What is one anxiety you have about the future, and how do you deal with it?

Affirmation Questions

These are questions which invite group members to say positive things about each other. Often we form friendships which are meaningful to us, but we seldom say out loud to those people just what they mean to us and why we value them. During the last meetings of a group, affirmation becomes particularly appropriate.

Examples

What is one quality that you value or admire in one or more members of this group?

If you could give a special gift to each member of the group, what would it be, and why?

What spiritual gifts do you see present in one or more members of this group? How are those gifts being used in a helpful way?

What has been meaningful to you in this group?

How has this group been important or helpful to you?

What do you value especially about this group?

If you were called on to give a speech describing the good qualities of the members of this group, what would you say?

While group members are often reticent to say positive things about each other, this quality can often be seen in the life of Jesus and the apostles. They could see the good qualities in people and affirm those, thus helping people to recognize and value what God was doing within and through them. This type of affirmation can be very important in expressing feelings and in building a sense of belonging and being cared for.

Accountability Questions

These questions are asked when group members promise to work actively at living out the implications of their Christian faith. Such question should only be asked when people have chosen to make themselves accountable to fellow group members.

Examples

What do you believe God wants you to do this week, and when and how do you intend to do it?

What changes do you believe you should make in your habits or actions this week? How will you tackle these?

What Christian action will you attempt this week, and what help will you need to accomplish it?

What spiritual disciplines are you going to follow this week, and why?

How did you get on with your commitment from last week?

What success and what failure have you experienced this week in your attempt to follow Christ?

What relationship should you work on this week, and how will you do it?

How will you practice thankfulness to God this week?

How is the Spirit prompting you as a result of our Bible study? What will you do about it, and when?

How will you share the good news of the gospel this week, and with whom?

What prayer discipline do you intend to observe this week?

What is one responsibility that you have to fulfill this week, and how do you feel about it?

Adapted from *Using the Bible in Groups* by Roberta Hestenes, © Roberta Hestenes 1983. Adapted and used by permission of the Westminster/John Knox Press.

Friend Search

Each of us comes in contact daily with others who share similar interests. Put an * or check mark in each box that tells about you, and fill in the bottom row with things that tell about you (like "has a sister" or "speaks French"). To find out what you and others may have in common, ask group members to sign the boxes that tell something about them.

Now that you know what you have in common, share these mutual interests with a new friend.

has a record collection	can swim	likes to jog	likes to sing	likes to travel	likes to fish
drives a car	likes to shop	visited a foreign country	likes to read	likes to cook	likes movies
plays an instrument	has a computer	has a part-time job	collects something	is a class or club officer	likes to paint
has a hero	has a pet	likes sports	plays tennis	won an award	likes to draw
___	___	___	___	___	___

Enabling

In This Context, Enabling Is a Negative Concept

Enabling is anything that stands in the way of or softens the natural consequences of a person's behavior. Unknowingly, an enabler helps the one he cares for to continue his downward spiral of addiction. He continues to help even though his assistance is being abused. Helpers learn to rescue their friend or loved one from their responsibilities. Enabling prolongs the problem. Some examples are:

- covering up the behavior of your friend
- bailing him/her out of jail
- making excuses for him/her
- minimizing your friend's problem
- blaming yourself
- giving your friend one more chance, over and over again

Biblical Examples

First Kings 21 records the enabling behaviors of Jezebel. Her husband, King Ahab, became angry and pouted because Naboth would not sell him his vineyard. When Jezebel noticed Ahab and his sullen condition, she devised a deceitful plan that would get the vineyard for him and rescue him from his pouting spell.

Eli was an enabler. The writer of 1 Samuel writes, "his sons made themselves contemptible, and he failed to restrain them" (1 Sam. 3:13).

The prodigal son's father was not an enabler (see Luke 15:11–32). He did not rescue his son from his responsibilities. Luke writes (Luke 15:16), "but no one gave him anything." The son broke out of his delusion ("came to his senses"), recognized his sinful condition, and returned to his compassionate father.

The well-meaning intentions of an enabler strengthen the dependent person's denial and sincere delusion. Enabling behaviors become habit-forming. The dependent person needs the enabler to support his denial and deceit. This is frequently accomplished by making the enabler feel guilty by saying, "If you really love me you will . . ."

Scriptures That Warn Against Enabling

"My son, if sinners entice you, do not give in to them" (Prov. 1:10).

"A hot-tempered man must pay the penalty; if you rescue him, you will have to do it again" (Prov. 19:19).

Personal Boundaries

Codependent	Interdependent
I can fall in love with a new acquaintance.	I know that love is based on respect and trust; these take time to develop.
I talk at an intimate level at the first meeting.	I don't overwhelm a person with personal information. I allow trust to develop slowly.
I am overwhelmed by and occupied with a person.	I am able to keep my relationships in perspective and function in other areas of my life.
I let others define me.	I know who I am in Christ, and I am wary of people who want to remake me.
I let others describe my reality.	I believe my perception of reality is just as accurate as anyone's.
I let others determine what I feel.	I refuse to allow someone else to tell me, "You don't feel that way."
I let others direct my life.	I listen to opinions, but I make decisions for myself based on God's leading of my choices.
I violate personal values to please others.	I am not willing to "do anything" to maintain a relationship. I have values that are not negotiable.
I don't notice when someone else displays inappropriate boundaries.	I am wary of someone who wants to get too close to me too soon. I notice if someone has values and opinions.
I don't notice when someone invades my personal boundaries.	I notice when others try to make decisions for me, are overly helpful, and/or do not consult me about time commitments.

From *Counseling Adult Children of Alcoholics* by Sandra D. Wilson, Ph.D. Copyright © 1989. Reprinted by permission of Word Books, Dallas, TX.

How to Receive Christ

1. Admit your need *(that you are a sinner)*.
2. Be willing to turn from your sins *(repent)*.
3. Believe that Jesus Christ died for you on the cross and rose from the grave.
4. Through prayer, invite Jesus Christ to come in and control your life through the Holy Spirit. *(Receive him as Savior and Lord.)*

What to pray . . .

Dear God,

I know that I am a sinner and need your forgiveness.

I believe that Jesus Christ died for my sins.

I am willing to turn from my sins.

I now invite Jesus Christ to come into my heart and life as my personal Savior.

I am willing, by God's strength, to follow and obey Jesus Christ as the Lord of my life.

Date _____   Signature _____

The Bible says . . .

"Everyone who calls on the name of the Lord will be saved." Romans 10:13

"To all who received him, to those who believed in his name, he gave the right to become children of God." John 1:12

"Therefore, since we have been justified through faith, we have peace with God through our Lord Jesus Christ." Romans 5:1

When we receive Christ, we are born into the family of God through the supernatural work of the Holy Spirit who lives within every believer. This process is called regeneration or the new birth.

Share your decision to receive Christ with another person.

Suggested Reading

Ackerman, Robert J. *Children of Alcoholics: A Guidebook for Educators, Therapists, and Parents.* Holmes Beach, Florida: Learning Publications, 1978.

Apthorp, Stephen P. *Alcohol and Substance Abuse.* Wilton: Morehouse-Barlow, 1985.

Augsburger, David. *Caring Enough to Confront.* Glendale: Regal Books, 1980.

Beattie, Melody. *Codependent No More.* New York: Harper and Row Publishers, 1987.

Benner, David G., ed. *Psychotherapy in Christian Perspective.* Grand Rapids: Baker Book House, 1987.

Carnes, Patrick. *Out of the Shadows: Understanding Sexual Addiction.* Minneapolis: CompCare Publishers, 1983.

Cook, Jerry, Stanley C. Baldwin. *Love, Acceptance and Forgiveness.* Glendale: Regal Books, 1979.

Crabb, Lawrence J. *Effective Biblical Counseling.* Grand Rapids: Zondervan Publishing House, 1977.

————. *The Marriage Builder.* Grand Rapids: Zondervan Publishing House, 1982.

Crowley, James F., ed. *Alcohol and Drugs: Working with Adolescents and Schools.* Minneapolis: Community Intervention, 1981.

————. *Alliance for Change.* Minneapolis: Community Intervention, 1984.

Griffin, Em. *Getting Together: A Guide for Good Groups.* Downers Grove: InterVarsity Press, 1982.

Hadaway, Kirk C., Stuart A. Wright, Francis M. Dubose. *Home Cell Groups and House Churches.* Nashville: Broadman Press, 1987.

Hart, Archibald. *Counseling the Depressed.* Dallas: Word Publishing, 1987.

Hemfelt, Robert, Frank Minirth, Paul Meier. *Love Is a Choice: Recovery for Codependent Relationships.* Nashville: Thomas Nelson Publishers, 1989.

Hestenes, Roberta. *Using the Bible in Groups.* Philadelphia: The Westminster Press, 1983.

Johnson, Vernon E. *I'll Quit Tomorrow.* San Francisco: Harper and Row Publishers, 1980.

Lee, Jimmy Ray. *Behind Our Sunday Smiles: Helping Those with Life-controlling Problems.* Grand Rapids: Baker Book House, 1991.

Malony, H. Newton, Thomas L. Needham, Samuel Southard. *Clergy Malpractice.* Philadelphia: The Westminster Press, 1986.

May, Gerald G. *Addiction and Grace.* San Francisco: Harper and Row Publishers, 1988.

McDowell, Josh, Dick Day. *Why Wait?* San Bernardino: Here's Life Publishers, 1987.

Miller, J. Keith. *Sin: Overcoming the Ultimate Deadly Addiction.* San Francisco: Harper and Row Publishers, 1987.

Minirth, Frank, Paul Meier, Robert Hemfelt, Sharon Sneed. *Love Hunger.* Nashville: Thomas Nelson Publishers, 1990.

Minirth, Frank, Paul Meier, Richard Meier, Don Hawkins. *The Healthy Christian Life—The Minirth-Meier Clinic Bible Study Guide.* Grand Rapids: Baker Book House, 1988.

Minirth, Frank, Paul Meier, Siegfried Fink, Walter Byrd, Don Hawkins. *Taking Control.* Grand Rapids: Baker Book House, 1988.

O'Gorman, Patricia, Philip Oliver-Diaz. *Breaking the Cycle of Addiction.* Deerfield Beach: Health Communications, 1987.

Parker, Bob. *Small Groups: Workable Wineskins.* Cincinnati: Christian Information Committee, 1988.

Peck, M. Scott. *People of the Lie.* New York: Simon and Schuster, 1983.

Rowland, Cynthia Joye. *The Monster Within: Overcoming Bulimia.* Grand Rapids: Baker Book House, 1984.

Sowder-Capell, Kathy and others. *Co-Dependency: An Emerging Issue.* Pompano Beach: Health Communications, 1984.

Stanley, Charles F. *Handle with Prayer.* Wheaton: Victor Books, 1988.

Sweeten, Gary R. *Apples of Gold Teacher's Manual.* Cincinnati: Christian Information Committee, 1983.

Thurman, Chris. *The Lies We Believe.* Nashville: Thomas Nelson Publishers, 1989.

VanVonderen, Jeff. *Good News for the Chemically Dependent.* Nashville: Thomas Nelson Publishers, 1985.

Vath, Raymond E. *Counseling Those with Eating Disorders.* Waco: World Books, 1986.

Ward, Charles G., ed. *The Billy Graham Christian Worker's Handbook.* Minneapolis: WorldWide Publications, 1984.

Wilson, Sandra D. *Counseling Adult Children of Alcoholics.* Dallas: Word Publishing, 1989.

Turning Point is a training program designed to help your church reach out to people at various phases of life-controlling problems This is accomplished through a systematic program which gives training, support, and a framework to a group of lay people in your church.

With practical curriculum based solidly on Scripture, Turning Point materials will keep your small groups on track.

If you wish to have a Turning Point Seminar in your church or community, contact Jimmy Ray Lee, P.O. Box 22127, Chattanooga, TN 37422-2127.